Customer Service is DEAD:

Delivering 6-Star Service In A 1-Star World

Mitche Graf

Cover Design: Ryan Lause

Back Cover Photo: Tami Graf

Line Editing: Free Eagle Studios, LLC

Publisher: Power Marketing 101

P.O. Box 405

Aurora, Oregon 97002 USA

ISBN: 978-1-7320344-6-4

Table of Contents

This book is dedicated to my 5-year old border collie, Tilly, who was by my side the entire time while I was writing this book. Through good days, bad days, and so-so days, she never failed to give me her unconditional love that I needed to get me through the finish line. Her separation anxiety and obsessive-compulsive disorder prevented her from leaving my side for more than 3 minutes at a time, and for that I am eternally grateful. (Plus, I've already dedicated other books to my wife and my three children!)

So, to man's best friend, I say thank you. Now, go get the ball!

Dad

About Your Captain For This Flight

Daddy of 3, best-selling author, serial entrepreneur, international-renowned business speaker, nationally-syndicated radio show host and former All-American Track & Field athlete Mitche Graf has been a passionate serial entrepreneur for over 25 years, dangling his toes into the ponds of many intriguing industries along the way.

From selling used bicycle parts out of his garage in the seventh grade to running four companies today, he has prided himself on knowing how to squeeze every drop of potential out of his endeavors.

In the middle of all of this, he managed to find time to become President for a Class A affiliate of the world-champion San Francisco Giants baseball team for a season and undertook an organizational re-brand which culminated in a 12% increase in attendance, one of the best in all of professional baseball in 2019.

In 2020, he launched *Business Edge Radio* and the *Business Edge Minute* podcast, and they quickly were picked up for national syndication on terrestrial radio. Both shows can be heard on radio stations across the United States as well as in podcast form on all platforms.

Over the past three decades, Mitche has created two award-winning restaurants, a bustling catering & events company, a national spice manufacturing business with over 4000 accounts, a photography studio, a cribbage board company, an award-winning limousine business, a portable hot tub rental business, a drive-through espresso company, an educational products company, an athletic fitness testing corporation, and even a night crawler company.

Having started, built, and successfully operated numerous enterprises in a multitude of industries has taught him a simple truth: the same basic business principles apply, regardless of the arena you may play in.

As an educator and motivational speaker, Mitche's high-voltage seminars and workshops have been delivered around the world to over 75,000 people in nine countries and nearly every state in the U.S. His cutting-edge articles and columns have appeared in the pages of business trade magazines such as *Rangefinder, PPA Magazine, Limo Digest, Chauffeur Driven, Image Maker,* and *Fresh Cup*, as well as many online marketing sites and blogs.

Customer Service Is DEAD: Delivering 6-Star Service In A 1-Star World is Mitche's 9th book. His other books include:

- *Marketing Your Espresso Business (1994)*
- *Power Marketing, Selling & Pricing (2004)* - Best Seller
- *The Passionate Life- A Common Man's Dream To Getting Anything You Want Out Of Everything You Do (2009)*
- *The Unleashed Entrepreneur: A KickAss Guide To Harnessing Your Inner Ninja, Working Less, & Building The Lifestyle Of Your Dreams (2018)* - Best Seller
- *BBQ Unleashed Recipe Book (2018)*
- *High Voltage Branding: Go From Ordinary To Extra-Ordinary (2020)*
- *The Business Basics BootCamp: The Ultimate Crash Course (2020)* - Best Seller
- *Entertain Like A Pro: Appetizers (2020)*

Most of his education and training has been from the School of Hard Knocks, from which he has earned his PhD degree. Through the high-notes of his business home runs, to the low-notes of bankruptcy in the 1990s, Mitche has continued to make bold attempts to redefine the limits of his abilities, and to reinvent the way his businesses operate so they don't become all-consuming black holes that suck him dry of his creative juices and zest for life.

Getting punched in the face from failure is probably the best teacher he has ever had and most of the lessons he has learned were born out of those failures.

He passionately believes life is meant to be lived, not endured, and we each can make a profound difference in the world. He loves his family, loves his friends, and the rest just falls into place!

Mitche is passionate about the outdoors, laughing, playing guitar, reading, listening to great music, cooking and eating, drinking good wine, taking a tremendous amount of time off to chill, and most importantly, spending time with his family.

Living in a small country town in Oregon allows him to raise his children the way he was raised...with a hard work ethic and a strong sense of community. He lives with his wife Tami and their three small children Jaycee, Colton, and Sierra, Tilly & Delilah the Dogs, Coral the Hermit Crab, Opa the Lizard, as well several hundred guppies (names not important).

He spends much of his time looking for ways to work smarter, not harder, so he can spend more time doing and enjoying the things in life that are most important to him. He believes that *EVERY DAY IS A SATURDAY*, and this perspective inspires him to wake up every day with a sense of excitement and enthusiasm to live his life by design.

Introduction

It was the trip of a lifetime.

My 13-year old son, Colton, and I were headed down to Arlington, Texas to watch a World Series game between our Los Angeles Dodgers and the Tampa Bay Rays. When the alarm sounded at 3:00 AM, we were both fired up and ready to go. It must have been the adrenaline that was pumping through our bodies.

We had been to the World Series before but left disappointed. If you are a sports fan, you know the feeling that I'm talking about. The pain is real and palpable, and the only thing that heals it is the start of the next season. The Dodgers had lost 2 of the last 3 World Series, and the thought of another loss was on the minds of every Dodger fan in the universe.

But we knew that this year was different. THIS was our year, and nothing was going to stop us! I even packed my 32-year-old t-shirt that I had purchased in 1988 when the Boys in Blue last won it all.

It had been worn through every playoff win and every playoff loss, then put back into the closet to live in total darkness until the next season came around. I always thought it was supposed to bring the team good luck, but I was beginning to question its importance. Could the t-shirt be the reason why they hadn't won it all? Only time would tell.

Once we got past security at the Portland International Airport, we headed to the Delta Sky Lounge so I could get a good cup of coffee and both of us could grab a little breakfast. Colton had not flown in quite some time and had forgotten what it was like to travel in style. Everything was new and exciting for him, and I found myself living each moment through his eyes.

The Alaska Air flight from the Pacific Northwest down to Dallas, Texas was just about as perfect as it could be and the excitement that I could sense from Colton gave me a shot of energy as well.

Colton was in complete awe over the little things that you and I may take for granted...the surge of adrenaline at take-off, the view from above the clouds, and the Biscoff cookies that are given out for free.

"Dad, these are the best cookies I've ever had!" he said. "Do you think I can ask for some extra packets so I can share with the rest of the family when we get home?"

"I'm sure the flight attendant would be happy to give you a big pile of them that you can stick in your bag," I assured him.

The next time our flight attendant stopped by, Colton asked if it would be okay for him to have a couple more packets to take with him. She obliged and gave him a large pile. He was over-the-moon happy and felt like this was going to be the best day of his life.

After an in-flight movie and some more Biscoffs, we landed at Dallas-Fort Worth Airport and ordered up an Uber. Up to this point, everything about our day was perfect. The impeccable service that we had received at every touch point had been nothing short of incredible.

We then headed outside to meet our ride. Within seconds of us reaching the pick-up point, our Uber pulled up and we loaded up for our 20-minute trip.

We were on our way!

After a brief hello, we realized that our driver did not speak fluent English. We had a difficult time understanding what she was saying, but we managed to agree that we were headed to the hotel next to the stadium. We sat back and began to talk about what a perfect day it had been so far while we looked at the sites along the way.

Within a minute of pulling away from the curb, our driver got lost inside of the maze of airport roads. She stared at her GPS app intently while she drove around in circles looking for the correct exit to take.

I asked if she had been to the airport before. Her response was indiscernible, so I leaned forward and looked at her phone. I hoped that I would be able to lend a helping hand in finding the correct road to take.

I asked very politely if she could please put her phone in a cradle or on her dash so she could drive with both hands, but she didn't seem to understand my request.

Ten minutes and two more wrong turns later, we were finally out of the airport maze and on our way. Colton and I giggled about getting lost twice inside of the airport, then began a 20-minute talkathon about how great the day had been, minus the short hiccup we had just been through.

When we finally came up for air, I started to look around for the stadium, but only saw flatlands and very few buildings. When we were leaving the airport, I didn't feel the need to plug the address into my own GPS because I was raised to automatically trust people, even strangers. I had never questioned a cab or Uber driver's directions and had always trusted that I would get to my destination. This approach had seldom failed me in all my life, but I soon found myself wishing that I had used my GPS.

It was a cloudy day, so I couldn't tell where the sun was and which direction we were headed. I asked the driver where we were, and her response did not make sense to neither Colton nor myself.

I then entered the hotel address into my phone and discovered that we were headed in the opposite direction! After several minutes of back-and-forth with the driver, she finally realized that we were indeed headed in the wrong direction and took the next exit so she could turn around.

We were now 45 minutes away from the hotel.

All the while, our driver stared intently at her cell phone instead of the road. I asked her once again to please put the phone down while she was driving, but she either didn't understand my request or simply chose to ignore it.

Colton, who had been silent while I tried to figured things out with the driver, finally chimed in and said:

"Dad, this is turning out to be a terrible day. Everything is ruined. We should call Uber and complain about the bad service we received. We should use Lyft the next time and never use Uber again."

As a father who has tried to raise my children with a "the glass is half-full" approach to life, I saw this as a teaching opportunity:

"Son, this is only a small hitch in our giddy up, and our day is still perfect. When we go to bed later tonight, I promise you that we will look back at this moment right now, and we'll laugh about it. It will be a small part in our overall experience, and we will look back fondly. It will just be a part of the Graf Boys Adventure."

While those words were coming out of my mouth, I could see them go in one of Colton's ears and out the other. In his mind, this was a major setback. In my mind, it was only a minor delay in what was overall going to be the best trip of his life.

The difference was that I had 58 years of life experience to draw upon, and he had 13. Not really a fair fight. His instant dislike for Uber was obvious and was potentially going to stick with him for the rest of his life.

On the 45-minute trip to the hotel, I could sense that Colton's mood had shifted slightly and was now a bit more positive.

"You know Dad, you're right," he said. *"This really has been a perfect day, and we shouldn't let our Uber ride ruin our trip."*

We then decided that NOTHING was going to stop our day from being one of the best days ever!

Even with our newfound positivity, our driver still managed to take two more wrong turns on the way to our hotel, but it didn't matter. We were determined to not let anything take away from our experience.

At long last, we made it to our hotel in one piece and got settled into our room, only to turn right around and take another Uber down to the ballpark to check out everything that was going on. We were going to the game on the following day, but just wanted to check out the brand-new stadium that was the talk of the baseball world and maybe grab some Texas BBQ.

This time, I checked the ratings of our driver before clicking "reserve." With over 5,000 5-star reviews, we were confident that we would not encounter the same issues as before. And this time, our driver not only delivered but exceeded our expectations.

When he arrived at the hotel, he got out to open our door and greeted us with an authentic Texas smile! His car was not only clean, but he had magazines in the backseat compartment for us to browse, there were hand sanitizers for us to use, and the professionalism of the driver was second to none. He recommended places we could eat, activities we could do before and after the game, and even chatted with us about our mutual love for baseball.

Before we knew it, we were at the ballpark and our Uber adventure was over, at least for the time being. I shook the man's hand and told him how much I appreciated him and his great service. My son commented how great he thought the driver was and how he wished all drivers were like that.

If the first driver had a pleasant demeanor and been able to drive us from the airport to the hotel without getting lost, she would have met our expectations and received a 5-star rating from us with a healthy tip. That's just what we do today when a business "meets" our expectations.

I didn't have the nerve to or the time to make our misadventures a big deal, as I realized that she probably depended on her income to pay her bills and support her children. The only thought I had was that she probably would do better in a different industry!

Then, I considered the service and experience we received from the 2nd driver. He not only met my expectations, he exceeded them by miles and miles. It didn't seem fair that I was only able to give him five stars. It would seem to me that when a company blows your expectations out of the water, you should be able to give more than five stars. Sounds reasonable to me.

When we have contact with a company, we have a certain level of expectation for the service we receive. We may not expect top-shelf service every time, but we do expect a minimum level of professionalism, courtesy, and understanding.

This book will give you a fresh set of eyes for what it means to provide your customers with what I call a ***"6-Star Experience,"*** and will shatter your current definition of what good service really means. It will give you a new way of looking at what the rules are for taking care of your customers. The game has changed drastically in the last few years, and you'll have to change with it or be left on the side of the business highway to wither away.

Now, let's get to work!

Chapter 1

The Death And Rebirth Of Customer Service

Traditional customer service **(CS)** in the business world is officially DEAD! We are now in a world that demands things faster, more conveniently, & cheaper, and many consumers are willing to forgo their demands to be taken care of at a high level.

The customer experience **(CX)** has been reduced to a website, a phone tree, and robotic employees who have been given extraordinarily little training on how to do their job correctly.

If we go to the drive-thru to get our morning caffeine and only must wait 20 minutes in line to get our $5 latte and a forced smile from the barista, we are happy and tip them a couple bucks.

If we only have to wait on hold for 10 minutes to talk with our banker about getting a new car loan, we feel fortunate. And if our server at our favorite restaurant only must be reminded twice about refilling your water, it's a great day!

Long gone are the days when you pulled into a "Service Station" to get gas and were met by a wonderful smile and a statement like the following:

"Good morning, can I fill your car up today with our premium-grade gasoline so that your engine works more efficiently? And while you're here, I'll check the fluids under the hood, look at your tire pressure, and clean your windshield while you wait."

We would pull in for gas and be treated to a vast plethora of unexpected services that were provided for free.

When I was a teenager, I would go to the service station on the corner next to my high school just because I thought it was fun to watch the employees work, but I would only go to that station when I needed gas. I was loyal to the people that worked there, loyal to the brand name, and addicted to the feeling that I got whenever I would pull in. It made me feel special and valued. To this day, I still go get the same brand of gas because of my memories of days gone by.

Today, we pull into the gas station, get out of the car, pay for our gas, and pump it ourselves. If we want our windshield washed or our oil checked, we're on our own. And if we are paying cash, we must go inside and wait in line to prepay. If our car doesn't take all the money that we paid, we must go back in and stand in line again just to get the change. If we get a smile and a thank you, those are complete bonuses.

By the time we get back in our car to leave, we feel stressed and rushed, not to mention smelly from the gas on our hands.

As the digital revolution continues to take root in our culture, so has the decrease in the importance of having actual humans at the front lines of a business. The Internet has taken away much of the human interaction that just a few short years ago was vitally important to the survival of a business.

Shopping for groceries, buying a movie ticket, making a phone payment to our insurance agent, or simply stopping at the bank to make a deposit are all touch points when we have the opportunity to talk to a frontline employee during our purchase. I call anyone who has direct contact with a customer at any point in the process a "Customer Experience Ambassador" **(CEA)**.

If I'm not greeted with at least a short and friendly hello or some eye contact, I have no problem telling them to not forget to greet their customers. It's not that I expect to have a real conversation but do expect to at least be shown a little consideration since I'm the one paying their wage!

It drives my wife and kids crazy when I do it, but it's something I feel strongly about. Most retail businesses depend on having their frontline folks represent their brand at the highest levels, but that skill has not been given the importance that it once had. It is becoming a dying art. And when the Internet began taking over every aspect of our lives, the importance became even more expendable.

If you are even a little like me, you feel the same way. We expect to have a basic level of service when we have some sort of interaction with a business. If they get it right, they continue to get our support. If they blow it, we will be happy to tell our friends and family about our bad experience. In person or online, it doesn't matter.

There's a new customer service benchmark study by SuperOffice that shows several alarming trends. Here are some key findings:

★ 62% of companies do not respond to customer service emails AT ALL.

★ 90% of companies do not acknowledge or inform the customer that an email has been received AT ALL.

★ 97% of companies do not send a follow up email to customers to see if they are satisfied with the response AT ALL.

★ Only 20% of companies can answer questions in full during the first contact.

★ The average response time to handle a customer service request is 12 hours and 10 minutes.[1]

No wonder so many customers have become jaded and have such a high level of discontent! Businesses are not even taking them seriously enough to take care of them on a basic level.

The good news? We have lots of room for improvement.

When you hear about the accolades of the best hotels and restaurants around the world, you typically hear about the "5-Star" ratings that they have. To them and the customers they serve, that means they are the absolute best at what they do.

5-Stars is the equivalent of Two Thumbs Up for a movie, or 100% on Rotten Tomatoes. Basically, it means that a business can't do any better in taking care of its customers.

Before we make a purchasing decision, small or large, many of us will take a quick look at the reviews of companies before making our final decision. If we see a series of 5-star reviews, it builds some trust, and we are happy to become a customer. If we see a spattering of 1-star or 2-star ratings, we skip to the next business. It's the way of the world these days. Social proof has become the driving force for many businesses who want to grow their sales and attract new customers.

Strangely, nearly 90% of us do NOT leave any sort of reviews for products or services we have purchased, but most of us rely on the reviews of others to help us with our buying decisions.

Let's take the 5-Star rating concept for a little walk around the block.

It's Friday night and you decide to order delivery for your family of 5. Everybody votes on

Chinese, so you visit the Internet to take a look at the menu for Happy Family Chinese Restaurant, which is your family's favorite. The website is professionally done, the menu is simple to understand, and the phone number is front and center.

When you call, the phone is answered right before the 2nd ring by a happy voice. After you place your order, the person on the phone gives you a total and says that your food will be there in 30 minutes. You say thank you and hang up the phone.

Thirty minutes later, there's a knock on the door. When you open it, you are greeted by a well-dressed young man. You pull out four twenties, hand the money to the driver, tell him to keep the change, and say thank you. He gives you one last smile as he tells you to have a good evening and enjoy the food.

The smells that are coming out of the bag are making you even more hungry than you already were, and you are ready to dive in. Your family devours their food in no time flat, you each read your fortune cookie, and all agree that everything was good.

Now, most people would say that this service deserves 5-stars. Would you agree? There was nothing about the experience that went sideways, and everything was exactly as you expected.

So, let's break this down a bit further.

- ★ **5-Star** service means you met my expectations, and everything went as expected. Nothing more, nothing less.
- ★ **4-Star** service means you may have met my expectations, but maybe the driver was 10 minutes late.
- ★ **3-Star** service means you kind of met my expectations, but the driver was 10 minutes late, and my food was cold.
- ★ **2-Star** service means you didn't really meet my expectations, the driver was 10 minutes late, my food was cold, and the person on the phone was a little rude.
- ★ **1-Star** service means you didn't meet my expectations at all, the driver was 10 minutes late, my food was cold, the person on the phone was a little bit rude, AND I didn't even like the food!

I've heard people even say that they would have given a business a 0-Star review if that was an option, which should make ANY business owner cringe.

As I mentioned earlier, only around 10% of customers will actually leave a review for a business, but nearly 100% of us will look at reviews when deciding on a making a purchase. To me, it sure seems that there isn't any way to reward a business if they go above and beyond our expectations.

Here's a few things to think about:

- What if when you called the restaurant, they called you by your first name because your name came up on their caller ID?
- What if they included complimentary egg flower soups with your order?
- What if the driver showed up in 20 minutes instead of 30?
- What if when you answered your door, the driver once again used your first name when he handed you the bags?
- What if he also gave you a $5 gift card that was good towards your next family dine-in date night?

* What if they sent you an email the next day with a video for a recipe that you can try at home?

* What if they sent you a special "Happy Birthday" card with signatures from all the employees?

* What if you when you ordered the fixins from them for your annual holiday party at your office, their staff spent extra time helping you set everything up just to help out?

Now, none of this is rocket science or difficult, but I think we all can agree that we would feel exceptionally good about doing business with this company.

In fact, I venture to say that we would consider ourselves BIG fans and would probably let friends and co-workers know about how great they are to do business with. This company will have earned the coveted and mystical 6th star in our book.

So, here's your challenge. Grab yourself a pen and paper, a good cup of coffee, and hit the easy chair. I want you to do these 3 things:

First, I want you to put yourself in the shoes of your perfect customer and look at your business from their perspective, NOT yours. We all tend to get stuck in ruts when it comes to making the CX the best it can be.

Evaluate every aspect of the CX when someone comes into your business, visits your website, or finds some other point of contact. While you are doing this, you should find some areas that perhaps aren't as efficient and customer-centric as they could be, which is incredibly good news.

The other part of this first step is to bring your customers into the project. What do they love about your company, what do they not love about you, and what suggestions can they give on ways to improve their experience with you? This can be as simple as picking up the phone and calling a small handful of your customers that you feel will give you honest feedback.

Another way is to have customer satisfaction surveys available for people to fill out, whether it be in person or online. If you already have surveys, great! If not, try to develop a short questionnaire that will provide you with valuable information. Once you receive them, you'll have two data sets: your own perspective, and that of your customers.

Second, I want you to write down what would make *YOU* an avid fan of your business. Don't put any limitations on what your mind spits out. Write it all down!

- ★ What would it take for your business to earn that magical 6th star?
- ★ Which of your systems are causing you the biggest headaches when it comes to having a smooth relationship with your customer?
- ★ Is there a need to completely break those systems down into the smallest number of moving pieces, then rebuild them with fewer moving pieces?
- ★ Do you have clear service expectations that are communicated clearly to staff and customers?
- ★ When speaking with customers, do you listen more than you talk?
- ★ Do you deliver more than the customer needs?

* Do you respond quickly to customers? Do you have metrics around response time?
* Do your people know your products and services deeply?
* Do you have a way to measure what they know?
* Do you have a list of customer needs that your products solve?
* Do you have a clear chain of command and protocol to follow when addressing customer concerns?
* Do you have any product or service that causes consistent confusion or questions for customers?
* Do you have guidelines around resolving customer issues?
* Do you regularly discuss how to behave professionally and politely with customers?

Lastly, I want you to begin the work of re-creating the CX from the ground up. I realize that this may take some time, serious evaluation, and possibly some additional resources to complete, but it's important that you begin the process NOW.

This book will give you many actionable techniques that can be implemented into your every touchpoint of the CX and will give you a new set of eyes when it comes to providing impeccable service.

Make a plan, set some goals on how you are going to measure your progress, and begin the work of creating an atmosphere around your business that allows your customers to have a 6-Star feeling each and every time they have some sort of contact with you.

If you keep this philosophy in the front of your mind in everything that your business does, I can guarantee that you will revolutionize your entire mindset. Before long, you will find yourself growing by leaps and bounds!

Is Customer Service Really DEAD?

Those were the days...

You know you're getting old when you start a sentence off with those words. Nostalgia can be a tricky thing and memory can be deceptive, but I do remember the days before CS died.

Grocery stores didn't have long lines for self-checkouts. There were real people who checked you out. Sometimes, they gave you coupons or even suggested better bargains in the store. They might even hold your place in line while you ran and got their suggestion or better yet, they'd send someone to get it. We all love the self-checkouts when we only have a couple of items, but many stores have nearly as many of self-serve stations as they do "manned" stations. The personal touch is being removed from our lives inch by inch.

Or how about dealing with your favorite online business? If you had a question about one of the items you were thinking about purchasing, there was a phone number listed on every page that encouraged you to give them a call. Today, you must send out a search party to find a phone number or an email address. Companies have attempted to build websites that are completely automated, meaning that you can't have any contact with a real person, even if you wanted.

When I was a kid, I can remember heading downtown to local department stores like Thrifty and JCPenney. You'd walk in and be greeted instantly. No matter what question you had there was someone to answer it. There were lifelong salespeople trained in their special domain to help with any issue you had; the appliance guys could fix your stuff if it went bad, and the tool guys could give you instructions on whatever project you could dream up. Home Depot and Lowe's have this figured out today and spend a tremendous amount of time and money training their team members to be able to provide an enjoyable and educational CX.

My favorite spot was the little popcorn kiosk located at the back of Thrifty's. The lady behind the counter was always willing to give me a bag, even if I wasn't spending any money. Just enough to keep me occupied while mom shopped.

Then, something started happening over the years. The focus of business turned away from people to profits. Employees became easily replaced by a grumpy high schooler who knew nothing about any of the products. It was a race to the bottom with prices because the belief was consumers only cared about price. Nothing else mattered.

So, what happened that took our focus off the one person that really mattered in business?

Employees Became Numbers

The death of CS didn't begin with ignoring the customer. It started with minimizing people. Employees became the largest item on the balance sheet and the easiest place for a company to cut expenses quickly.

By eliminating the best people and replacing them with unskilled, untrained people, companies sent a signal to their employees that people didn't matter. Employees translated this to mean customers didn't matter. If I am expendable, what good is a customer? Company culture became diffuse with poor attitudes toward people because all that mattered was cutting costs and increasing profits.

Unfortunately, the public responded with fervor at the lower prices and were willing to ignore the poor service. Eventually, there was no out.

The Public Became Passive

The average consumer wasn't ignorant to the changes. At first, their wallets rejoiced, and they embraced the new changes of self-service and low prices. Then, they forgot.

They expected poor service. Some complained, but it fell on deaf ears. This was the way business was run now. There was no fighting city hall, and people had to expect it.

Technology Replaced Human Interaction

In the 1980s, a new technology arose called Interactive Voice Response (IVR). IVR allowed digitized voice to be recorded on a hard drive. If your family had one of those fancy black boxes where you could record your voice for people to hear when you weren't home (or just didn't want to answer!), you were considered fancy. Interactive Voice Response also allowed a customer to input data back to the company with their numbers on their phone.

So, it worked like this. A customer called, and they heard a series of options from 1-to-5. The voice said option 2 was customer service, and that is what we wanted. We pushed 2 on our phones and went straight to a customer representative. This allowed companies to create "phone trees" to get callers to where they needed to go before interacting with them. It allowed us to get to the exact person who could help with our exact problem. Today, this technology is everywhere, and it has allowed companies to provide the perfect person to help the customer with whatever their reason was for the call.

It seemed like a great idea at the time, but companies of all sizes began outsourcing their call centers. With businesses dedicating entire floors to CS, cost effectiveness came into play. Outsourcing customer care to other countries who would do it less expensively became a common business practice by the early 1990s.

The real issue was that in cutting the cost of CS, companies alienated their consumers, never to return.

Customer Journey Mapping

Journey Mapping is an excellent tool to help visualize the customer journey they will experience with your business. By creating a map, you begin with the customer as a prospect even before they are aware of you. You take them along the journey until they purchase, and then follow them as they continue to interact with you as a long-term fan.

As you think about sketching out your customer's journey with your company, consider these tips:

* Make sure your map is a visual representation of the customer journey.

★ Use customer personas as the person in your map.

★ Represent the customer needs, feelings, goals, and pain points.

★ Put yourself in the customer's shoes.

★ Illustrate every step they take when engaging with your business.

★ Detail the full end-to-end CE from their perspective.

The purpose should be to provide valuable insight on who your customers are and how they experience your business. This document helps you see the world from your customer's point of view and allows you to take action based on any friction or pitfalls you find along the journey.

The Internet & Social Media

In the latter half of the 1990s, businesses discovered the Internet, which opened new avenues for reaching customers. We began to see a glimmer of hope and a small little light as companies were forced to think about the CX as a means of setting themselves apart from their new online competitors.

Brick & Mortar stores saw the threat, and realized human interaction was the only thing that made them different than their online competition. Talk of CS and CX became important once again.

Social media entered the picture in the late 2000s, and the customer became vocal in ways they couldn't before. They shared their good and bad experiences and weren't shy about expressing their opinions if things didn't go their way. Businesses were forced to listen to protect their reputations.

It appeared that CS and the CX were reborn. But sadly, most of us had forgotten how to do it along the way. Businesses had to relearn how to master great service all over again. Technology had been a boon and could help us craft that experience and accelerate convenience but could never again be a digital wall we hid behind.

This rebirth is at the heart of 6-Star Service.

Yes, we can have the most modern computers, the best software, and the most awesome smartphone app for reaching our customers. They are fantastic tools, and we recommend utilizing them. Yet how are we to know whether we have reached our customers to the extent that their needs are heard and applied to our business practices? We must go from mediocre to something very special.

And in doing that, we gain an edge. After looking at the best of the best of CS over the years, whether offline or online, 6 major points became clear to me on how to navigate this new environment we are living in. I think there needs to be a new level of CS, a new scale on how our customers judge us by. I suggest we add one more star to the scale for how businesses are judged.

Think of these 6-Stars as guideposts that will keep you on the right path as your transform your own organization into CS and CX superstars!

THE 6-STAR SERVICE MANIFESTO

DISCLAIMER: Achieving the 6th Star is a philosophy, a state of mind, a way of life, a manifesto that you adhere to when it comes to taking care of your customers. Once you have a firm grasp on this philosophy and understand it deeply, you will be able to apply it to every aspect of your business.

Here's a summary of each of the 6 Stars. Each one will have a special chapter with examples and practical ideas on crafting your own unique CS story.

Follow these 6-Stars and you will revolutionize your business, guaranteed!

I want you to imagine that you visit a website to place an order for a new TV for your family room. Or you go into your local big box TV store to find the perfect model. We all have different ways in which we make our purchasing decisions these days and have many options. Before you begin your shopping, whether it be online or in person, you see a sign that says the following:

We Believe In The 6-Star Service Manifesto

We Promise To:

Star 1: Do Our Very Best To ***"EXCEED"*** Your Expectations

Star 2: Treat You Like ***"GOLD"*** In Every Interaction

Star 3: Correct Our Mistakes ***"QUICKLY & EFFICIENTLY"***

Star 4: Create an Unparalleled Culture of Service ***"EXCELLENCE"***

Star 5: Build Our Relationship With You Based on Mutual ***"RESPECT"***

Star 6: Never Forget That ***"YOU"*** Are the Most Important Part of Our Business

How would that make you feel right off the bat? Would you feel like this company cared about you as a customer and valued your business? You absolutely would!

While I recommend reading the book straight through, feel free to jump ahead if you see a star that screams at you and get to work!

Customer Service Checklist

- ✓ Do we have clear service expectations that are communicated clearly to staff and customers?
- ✓ When speaking with customers, do we listen more than we talk?
- ✓ Do we provide more than the customer needs?
- ✓ Do we respond quickly to customers? Do we have metrics around response time?
- ✓ Do our people know our products and services deeply? Do we have a way to measure what they know?
- ✓ Do we have a list of customer needs that our products solve?
- ✓ Do we have a clear chain of command and protocol to follow when addressing customer concerns?

- ✓ Do we have any product or service that causes consistent confusion or questions for customers?
- ✓ Do we have guidelines around resolving customer issues?
- ✓ Do we regularly discuss how to behave professionally and politely with customers?

Chapter 2

Star 1: Do Your Best To Exceed Expectations

As consumers, we love to feel special. It's a feeling that never gets old, and it should be at the very center of how you take care of your customers.

Several years ago, we were attending an exceptionally large art and music event where we had long lines for days on end for our BBQ. On the 2nd day of the event, our sales were outrageous, and we could not keep up with the crowds.

As the day went on, we began to get low on coleslaw and didn't have an extra set of hands that could run down and pick up more, so I called the local Smart Food Service store and asked if anyone was getting off work soon to bring us down a few cases of coleslaw. Adrian, the GM, told me, "Mitche, I'll figure something out for you."

Forty-five minutes later, we were about to run out of coleslaw, but Adrian himself showed up soaked from head to toe with sweat (it was over 100 degrees that day) with a large box of tiny little bags of coleslaw. That was curious to me since the bags at his store were typically 5lbs each.

Then, he made me a customer for life.

"I knew it was important that you get more coleslaw, and we were completely out, so I went down to Safeway and bought everything they had," he said. "I hope that is ok."

It didn't matter that we only spent $150,000 a year on their products, he had to park about ½ mile away and walk with the heavy box in 100 degree weather, and it didn't matter that he had to leave his store in the middle of a rush to bring me product. All that mattered was that one of his customers had a problem, and he wanted to help solve it.

He had just saved what could have been a major disaster for us and creatively solved the problem. He was, and still is, my hero!

Can you think of an example of when a business went above and beyond your expectations? Maybe it was when the manager of your favorite restaurant had the Chef make a special dessert for your anniversary without you knowing it, that time when the landscaping company sent you a very thoughtful Thank You card for all your past business, or perhaps it was the time you accidentally broke the gold chain on your necklace and the jewelry store repaired it at no charge.

Going above and beyond what your customers expect from you is a sure-fire way of building customer loyalty and earn fans for life.

I have two mottos that I would like to share with you that may completely flip your approach to CS.

1. **What can I do today to make my customers' life a little bit better?**
2. **What does it hurt to give a little bit extra?**

Does that sound too simple? Maybe, but those 24 tiny words have the power to revolutionize the way you approach the CX.

After all, what does it hurt for us to give just a little bit more when it comes to providing an impeccable CX to our customers? Something not expected can often bring the biggest results. What can you do in your business that shows your customers that you care "just a little bit" more?

Back in the 70s, there was a band called Dr. Hook, and they cranked out some of the best love songs that this world has ever seen. If you haven't heard their music, I recommend checking them out on YouTube. One of their song's muses *"when you think I've loved you all I can, I'm gonna love you a little bit more"*.

Having a 6-Star mentality will not only revolutionize the way your business operates but will also give you a competitive edge in the market. What does it hurt to give just a little bit more?

80% of companies say they have great customer service, but only 8% of customers agree. When I work with companies on marketing and developing a value proposition, I always ask what makes them different than their competitors. Can you guess what they say?

"We have great customer service."

Everybody says that. Have you ever met a business that proudly proclaimed that it sucks at CS? No![23]

But when I ask what they mean by great CS, I get crickets chirping. The ones who give answers sound like the minimum expectations that every business should follow.

The first path toward great CS is exceeding your customers' expectations. We all know what it means to deliver on what we promise, but you must know your customer's expectations before you can blow their mind with exceptional service.

Know Your Customers

I can honestly say that my best customers are the ones that I have a personal relationship with and would even invite them over for a family BBQ.

I enjoy the process of getting to know all sorts of people and find it fascinating to learn all about them. There are so many cool life stories that people will share if they're asked. Building this sort of connection with people on a human level is the first step in getting to know what their wants and desires are. If you don't dig deep enough to find out, you will not be able to truly know how to meet and exceed their expectations.

When talking with customers and prospects, you need a three-fold goal.

- You want to know what you are doing well.

- ★ You want to know where you can improve.
- ★ You want to know what the customers' pain points are.

Knowing these three pieces of information are vital to understanding their thought process. It's also important that you ask open-ended questions so that you can learn about your customers.

Know Their Problems

Do you know how the best salespeople develop loyalty before the sale is even closed? *They find the customer's pain.*

The customer may not even be consciously aware of it, but the salesperson digs that pain out and places solutions for it before their eyes.

Do you have the investigative skills needed to find it? Just in case you are not convinced of the power of customer pain, here are several benefits that make the time digging worth it.

- ★ **Overcome objections.** Before the bulk of the sales process begins, objections become minimized because the customer realizes they have a problem that needs to be solved, and creating that pain gives an urgency to having it fixed.

- **Creates relationship wedge.** Their previous salesperson hasn't found the pain, or they wouldn't be talking with you. Immediately you get your foot in the door and begin questioning the relationship they have with their current salesperson.
- **Establishes credibility.** You know something others don't. You become credible. You have found something others haven't.
- **Expert status.** Before your product is shared, you should begin to be viewed as an expert, just because you know where their current product has failed them.

So, how do you find a person's pain?

Questions.

The best sales and service people listen more than they talk. They ask questions, and let the customer do the work.

It's not just any question that gets to the heart of a problem. Three types are needed the most.

1. **Stay Open** - Don't ask *"yes"* and *"no"* questions, or questions with one word responses. Ask open-ended questions like:

"How long have you been with Company X? Why are you considering leaving? What kind of experience have you had with Company X?"

You may have to ask a one word question, but always follow-up with an open ended question.

2. **Tell Me About It** - While not technically a question, nothing gets people talking more than this one statement.

CEA: *"What's your relationship like with Company X?"*

Customer: *"Good."*

CEA: *"Tell me about it."*

Before they realize it, they have expressed a frustration or disappointment, and this is where the gold is.

3. **Dig with the Why** - This may be the best question you can ask. Nothing fancy is needed. Just ask why? *Why are you shopping? Why is that*

important? Why don't you like...? Last question should always be *"Anything else?"*

So, you've mined the customer's problems and frustration, what's next?

- **Support It** - If you have found problems and frustrations that you can solve, support it with examples of your other CX and start your sales process.
- **Reject It** - Perhaps, you found someone that you know you can't satisfy. He is unreasonable, and you can't make him any happier than his current situation. It may be time to walk away. This is hard, but the maintenance of this customer may require more than you are willing to give.

Spend some time alone thinking through these strategies. Once you've done that, craft out sample questions and rehearse them in your brain until you know them like the back of your hand.

Don't Make Assumptions

You've heard the old saying about assumptions. They make us all look a little silly, but we assume things about what our customers think all the time. These assumptions can keep us from exceeding expectations, especially if we wind up under-delivering in the mind of the customer.

In a world where human interaction seems to be rare and at a premium, demand for an exceptional CX is at an all-time high, especially among millennials and Gen Z.

Microsoft found in 2017 that 54% of customers expect a higher level of service today compared to just one year prior. I'm sure that number has continued to go up since then.

Scan Social Media

Social Media can be a powerful medium for marketing and understanding your customers. Sites like LinkedIn are perfect for understanding your customer if you are in a B2B business, whereas Facebook, Instagram, and Pinterest can reveal customer insights if you're targeting consumers directly.

Forums, Amazon, and eBay provide a lot of methods for customer research. Enter your product on Amazon and read the reviews, good and bad, for similar products from your competitors. You will quickly learn what frustrates consumers and what wows them into wanting to buy more. This is a great exercise for Saturday morning with a good cup of coffee!

Regardless of what industry you are in, doing this kind of research is important to developing a top-shelf CX philosophy.

The Ideal Customer

When you begin thinking about your customer, your mind starts racing. If you are an aggressive businessperson, you probably think everyone needs your product, but step back for a moment and think about who your perfect customer is. Who do you want to do business with each day and have a long-term relationship with?

Sally is a hustler. She is an aggressive real estate person in her market. If you thought about Sally's customers, you would think that she services every type of home buyer out there, but that's not how Sally thinks.

Yes, Sally began her career with a shotgun approach to customer acquisition, but she couldn't accelerate her business until she honed-in on her ideal customer.

Sally eventually began focusing her marketing efforts on first-time home buyers. She knew the pains and struggles they went through and tried to make these buyers feel special.

Anyone who has spent time in a sales and service business often lives by the phrase the customer is always right, but are they? Is there a time when you might want to fire a customer?

Sometimes, you are better off saying no than to attempt to service a new customer who will only be a pain in your backside! It pays to know your customer and know yourself.

Think about Wal-Mart and Nordstrom. Stories abound about Nordstrom going above and beyond in the pursuit of delighting their customers. On the other hand, people rarely feel delight when leaving a Wal-Mart, yet both are extremely successful at what they do.

The difference is that they know their customers and themselves. Wal-Mart's goal is to bring products to consumers at the cheapest possible prices. Nordstrom wants to bring high-quality products to customers, creating an experience of luxury and excellence.

To succeed, you must do the same thing. This can be difficult to determine, but it becomes part of what defines your business and its brands in your community.

Have you done this? Do you know what your ideal customer looks like? If you are having trouble defining who that customer is, go negative!

Make a list of people you DON'T like doing business with or who you don't want to do business with. You will soon find that you are narrowing the scope of your customer quickly but will often find that there are people in that list that are making it into your business and frustrating you and your staff. It is time to put some stop signs in place against those you define as customer vampires draining the life from you and your business.

Leadership expert, Michael Hyatt, developed a matrix that helps identify your ideal customer:[4]

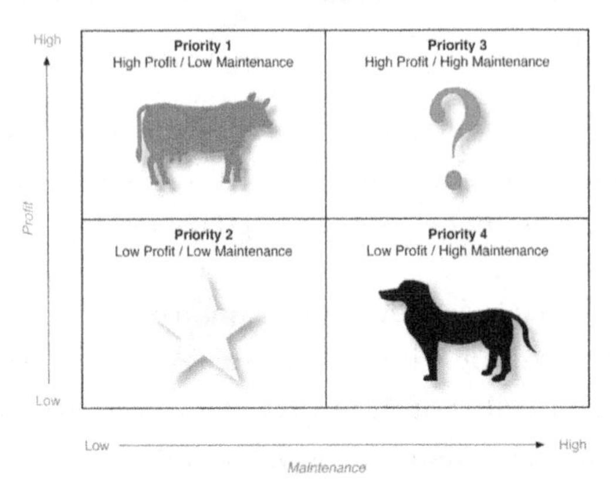

This chart will begin to help you refine who your ideal customers are, allowing you to create action steps around each type so that you can provide appropriate levels of delight and service.

Let's take each one from the lowest priority to the highest.

Priority 4: Low Profit/High Maintenance. These are the people who generate the least amount of revenue for you but create the most amount of work. They are never happy. They call with billing questions constantly, forever make demands of you, and offer little in return. You're giving way more value than they are, so you are better off eliminating them from your efforts.

Priority 3: High Profit/High Maintenance. These may really be the vampires inside your business. They generate a higher amount of revenue for you, but they are hard to deal with and drive your staff crazy. You secretly think about dumping them, but the benefits they bring keep you hanging on, suffering whatever abuse they continue to inflict upon you.

You may not let them all go but force yourself to determine whether the difficulty they offer is worth the value you receive from them.

Priority 2: Low Profit/Low Maintenance. This customer doesn't generate a lot of value for your company, but they are so easy to work with and create little friction in the office that you are willing to serve this type of customer all day long. Even though they don't pay much, a lot of them become valuable because they create so little work for you.

Priority 1: High Profit/Low Maintenance. This customer has a high return on investment. They generate a greater-than-average revenue per customer, are happy, pleasant, and create extraordinarily little work with your staff. They send referrals and never get petty or bog the office down with weird policy or billing questions.

You can't please everybody all the time, BUT you can choose who you want to please and build your business around that.

In the business world, many people use "Pareto's Principle" to determine where they spend their valuable time and resources. It suggests the following:

- 80% of your profits come from 20% of your customers.
- Conversely, 20% of your profits come from the other 80% of your customers.
- 80% of your efforts bring you 20% of your results.
- Conversely, 20% of your efforts bring you 80% of your results.
- 80% of your customer service issues come from 20% of your customer base.
- Conversely, 20% of your customer service issues come from 80% of your customer base.

Knowing this, wouldn't it make sense to figure out ways to develop strategies to attract new customers who fall into the Priority 1 category? Your Priority 4 customers can make it difficult to service your great customers, so it really is ok to let some of your customers go. You don't have to feel bad about it.

Modern Customer Expectations

Today's customer expects much more than in the past. There seems to be a memory of times when you could walk into a local store and managers and clerks knew your name and what you wanted. Somewhere along the way, we lost this, but customers have fought back. After years of faceless interactions, people crave human connections in commerce again.

Here's a quick list of expectations customers tell consumer research surveys that they expect:

1. Personalization. They want a shopping experience that is personal.

2. A quick resolution of transactions and problems.

3. The removal of friction from transactions.

4. They long for experts. There are so many options for customers today, and we can easily get paralyzed by choice and want someone to be the guide. Don't be afraid

to direct your customer to the right product or service.

5. Quality before efficiency. Most companies use speed as the ultimate customer service metric. Zappos, the online shoe store, is a perfect example here. They have built a business on expanding the happiness of the customer. When dealing with customer support, wouldn't you agree 15 minutes in heaven is always better than 5 minutes of frustration?

The problem is that speed is so easy to measure and quality customer interaction can be slippery and intuitive. You know when you get it, but it rarely can be paired down to a process-driven metric.

Needs vs Expectations

Needs are what customers want your product or service to do for them, and expectations describe how customers feel about their interaction with your company.

Think about my Uber example. I needed to get somewhere. The first driver eventually got me there, even though it wasn't as timely as I expected and there were obstacles in the way. The second driver anticipated an experience and made us feel like royalty on the journey. I can only imagine if they had gotten lost or sidetracked, they would have made an experience out of it for me and my son.

When we are anticipating needs, we are looking for a problem to solve.

To anticipate the needs of others is not a trick. It is a set of skills that we can hone into a sharp tool. Let's be clear here. We are not second guessing our customers or trying to solve all their problems. We are creating a space where we can solve some.

The best way to do this is to create a space where a customer can express and share their ideas. We often overlook the ideas of the customer because some of them will not apply to what we are selling or working on.

When we pay attention to the needs of our customers, we need only look to the front lines. A great CEA person will find that instinct is an unbelievably valuable tool, whether it is a subconscious feeling, or something based on wisdom and experience. No matter how instinct is derived, the needs of customers will likely change from person to person.

Know Your Business

Do you know your business from inside your customer's head? You probably have a great understanding of your financials and marketing. You even know your products and services so well you can recite the details in your sleep.

But have you looked at your products and services from your customers eyes? If you asked them to detail all the things you do, what would they tell you?

Discover what is unique about YOU and do that repeatedly!

Real World Examples

So, I dumped a lot of work on you, didn't I? Even with all the research and data you've accumulated to analyze your customers, sometimes you just need real world examples of what we mean.

Start with times in your life when you've been surprised by a company's interaction with you because it went above and beyond anything you could imagine. Exceeding exceptions is a surprise. It's so infrequent because we never expect it.

I recently had my car in the body shop to repair a small dent in the front fender. When I dropped the car off along with the keys, I inadvertently forgot to take off the master key to my office. By the time I figured this out, it was the end of the day, and I couldn't leave the building unlocked to go back to the body shop to get my master key.

My solution was to have a taxi go to the shop to pick up the key, then bring it to me. When I called the body shop to let them know about it, the GM said he would take care of making the arrangements.

About 20 minutes later, the GM himself walked into my office with the key! He drove all the way across town to fix a problem that I created, not him.

When the repairs were done, they delivered the vehicle to my office complete with a car wash and a deep cleaning. That level of service was not asked for nor expected, but it made me a customer for life!

Customer Experience Assessment Questions

Is your business focused on the customer experience?

A) No.

B) Yes, we understand it, but don't have any written plans around CX.

C) Yes, we track CX metrics and have action steps. It is not integrated with all our business channels.

D) Yes, we track metrics, have action steps, and every channel has a plan.

Do you know your customers?

A) No. We haven't done any surveys or research into our customers.

B) Yes. We have done research, but no written plans or actions.

C) Yes. We have a plan for understanding our customers.

D) Yes. We have a plan and have integrated it with every employee and channel.

Do you act on customer feedback?

A) No. We do not collect information.

B) We collect but have no action steps related to feedback.

C) Yes, we collect regular feedback, but don't have clear action plans in place for each piece of feedback.

D) Yes, we collect information and have processes to respond and evolve our processes for continual improvement.

Can customers easily engage with your company?

A) Yes, but only through email, phone, and contact forms.

B) Yes, we have multiple engagement points, but there is no thought to the customer experience.

C) Yes, but each channel has different processes that are not consistent to deliver superior customer experience.

D) Yes, customers can engage with us via a wide variety of contact points. The interaction is consistent, and customer experience is continually monitored.

Chapter 3

Star 2: Treat Customers Like Gold in Every Interaction

There's a show on Discovery that many of you have probably heard of called *Gold Rush*. It's a reality show about a bunch of guys who try to find enough gold in Alaska to make themselves rich. They have bulldozers, scoops, shaker boxes, dredges, dump trucks, refiners, gold pans, 4-wheelers, and lots of fuel to run all the machinery.

After moving hundreds of tons of dirt and rocks around for days and weeks on end, dealing with their equipment breaking down on a regular basis, and solving the constant in-fighting that the crews have, they are left with a bucket full of concentrates that they continue to reduce into just the gold that hopefully exists at the bottom.

They measure their success by how many ounces of gold they get at the bottom of the bucket. With gold near $2,000 per ounce as of this writing, it doesn't take much to make someone rich!

It then goes into a mason jar for safe keeping. The next day, they start all over again until Mother Nature begins her descent into winter and the season is over.

A mason jar full of gold is the Holy Grail for miners. Many men and women have died trying to *"strike it rich,"* yet few have succeeded. That doesn't stop people from trying, does it?

My father would take me gold panning in the Mojave Desert, so I know what it's like when you see a single spec of gold at the bottom of your pan. You actually get giddy about it, and it's easy to start dreaming about finding a jackpot of gold right under your feet. That's why they call it gold fever!

That mason jar represents the dreams of the crew and becomes the gateway to a better life. The gold miners will do anything to keep that gold safe and protected. It becomes their main focus, and all the efforts are built around the mason jar full of gold.

I want you to think about your most prized possession right now, such as precious metal, a portrait of a parent, or a letter you received from a dear friend. How does it make you feel when you think about NOT having it? Would it make you sad?

Would it make you change your behavior to get it back?

How would you do that? You treat them like gold, so they continue coming back again and again.

This is where many businesses fail. All their effort is focused on getting customers into the door the first time, but not keeping them there over the long-term. The process is not difficult once you raise every interaction to the gold standard.

If you don't treat your current customers well, someone else will. We all tend to become lazy once we've sealed the relationship with a sale. It's human nature to feel that way, but you must fight the urge to become complacent with your customers.

This is where *Gold Star Treatment* enters the picture.

Nordstrom has a reputation for treating its customers like gold. The most famous example of Nordstrom's commitment to service is from 1975. It's old, but their commitment to CS excellence remains.

A man returned to a store with 4 snow tires in the bed of his truck. He had bought the tires at a store several weeks prior, but he discovered that it had been replaced by a new Nordstrom.

Rather than leaving, he entered the store, and told his dilemma to a salesperson. The clerk allowed him to return the tires and then refunded him the money. Sounds like something that many businesses would do if needed. But just so you know, Nordstrom's has never sold tires, even back in 1975!

You might be confused at such a bad business decision, but it reflects the attitude of founder John Nordstrom who has said:

"Our commitment is 100% to customer service. We are not committed to financial markets, we are not committed to real estate markets, we are not committed to a certain amount of profit. We are only committed to customer service. If we make a profit, that's great. But customer service is first. If I'm a salesperson on the floor and I know that the people who own this place are committed to customer service, then I am free to find new ways to give great customer service. I know that I won't be criticized for taking care of a customer. I will only be criticized if I don't take care of a customer."

No one would argue that their commitment to CS has hurt their business. They are one of the few department stores have stuck around to this day. Sears and JCPenney have gone the way of the dinosaur, and their disappearance is directly tied to their abandonment of CS.

There are simple ways that your business can begin the process of treating customers like gold.

Be Courteous

Common wisdom states that *y*ou never get a second chance at a first impression. This is nowhere truer than CS. Treating people with courtesy and respect will go a long way toward making people feel valued.

Customer Service Begins With a Smile

We are only talking about at the start here. You do not have to hold a smile for the entire interaction.

Do it before any words are spoken. If you start speaking and then smile, something is lost. Many people do not trust someone who starts talking and then smiles. Our brains register it as a form of deception.

Our minds rarely reject a smile so long as it is first and genuine.

You may be thinking: *"But I am on the phone. How are they going to see my smile?"*

A smile does more than just make your customer relaxed; it also relaxes your CEA. Starting a conversation with a smile puts us in a mindset that makes it so that whomever we are in contact with is someone we care about. Caring can be expressed with a simple smile, even to someone on the phone.

So, we start with a smile. It may seem trivial, but there is nothing that a genuine smile and a little bit of skill can't solve.

Civility

Civility and politeness are not the same thing. The difference is caring. To be polite is to have good manners. Civilized is not Polite.

Consider that we are polite for a reason. We are socially conditioned by our families and other peers to either be polite or not. There is nothing to say that it isn't appropriate to offer a *"Thank you"* or *"You're welcome"* almost as a part of our base nature as humans. To be polite is far better for us psychologically than to be rude.

Being polite keeps things orderly, predictable, and comfortable, even when life feels the opposite of those concepts. It is polite to smile and nod when a friend says something cruel. We smooth over awkward moments and discomfort when it emerges.

Often, we pretend we do not hear anything and just keep going.

This is not civility.

The truth may be that this is the exact opposite of civility. Being polite may be a form of quiet violence. Consider that ignoring someone because you are polite may perpetuate oppression. It turns courtesy into a weapon that is used to ease social discomfort, possibly in a time and place where we need to be discussing it. Politeness may be the destruction of civility.

To be civil is to care for yourself and for others. We must overcome the uncomfortable to make sure everyone around us knows that we are caring. To be civil is to be an active part of society and the community.

Being polite is something you are. Civil is something you do. Until you put it into practice beyond words, being civil is not complete. We can all be polite to each other, which is something I believe we need to do much more of these days. To be a civil being should be a moral imperative.

We are not going to scream at our customers, clients, guests, or contractors. We are going to go beyond politeness and begin to practice caring. The difference between being an ordinary CEA and extraordinary representative is that you care for each one of your customers.

This gets extremely tiresome after you deal with more than a hundred people a day. It takes a person who knows how to care to get to our 6th Star. As employers, we need to train caring. The curse and beauty of caring are that it is individualized. Each company has a different way of showing they care.

Customer Well-Being

Creating a sense of customer well-being is all about anticipating customer needs and making customers feel good about doing business with you.

Warby Parker, the online eyewear company, crafted a business around customer well-being. Designer glasses are expensive, and after paying for an exam and lenses, most people must go cheap on frames. Warby Parker wanted to change that. They designed an online site for people to be able to get high-end eyewear below a hundred bucks.

Today, they have over 30 retail locations outside of their online shop. Once per quarter, every single employee works in a showroom or on the phone directly communicating with customers. By implementing this practice, the company as a whole has become more focused on the customer. To continue their mission toward well-being, they created a Buy a Pair, Give a Pair program. The program trains opticians in developing countries and then provides them with low cost glasses.[5]

It's not just companies that sell tangible products who can craft a commitment to well-being. Solutions for Progress, a financial coaching service firm in Philadelphia has provided charities and public agencies with tools that streamline low-income families' access to public benefits.

They created the Benefit Bank and MyBudgetCoach as tools to help the poor improve their financial standing. Organizations that serve the poor purchase licenses to customized versions of these programs.[6]

Memorable Environments

One way to treat customers like gold is to create a full-sensory CX. Sensory experiences don't just apply to brick and mortar stores. Online businesses can use digital assets to do the same thing.

Both offline and online businesses use email to communicate with customers, but most people who sign up for an email newsletter just have their inbox blasted with spam until they unsubscribe. This is a common tale.

How can you change that interaction?

If you can't create a warm and friendly environment, think about how to use humor or nostalgia. These are powerful tools that marketers have used in sales copy for years, and they motivate customers to loyalty.

Adopt a language that is unique to your business. LEGO uses the phrase "Happy Building" whenever they sign off a message by print or phone with a customer. Walgreens uses "Be Well" in all their customer interactions. Using unique language builds your brand and creates memories about you in the minds of your customers.

Smell triggers something in our brain like no other sense. Great realtors know this and will often place fragrant apples and freshly baked cookies when they have an open house. It warms people up and makes them remember the experience.

Another effective way to make memories is by focusing on the little details.

Disney is a master at this. Everything about what they do immerses you into their world. They pay such close attention to details that you probably don't even notice them. A couple of years ago, my family went on a vacation in our motor home up and down the West Coast, and the crown jewel was a trip to Disney Land.

While at Disney, we were transported somewhere different. The park was exceptionally clean, the cast members were all friendly, and they even embellish something as small as doorknobs to create an immersive experience for their guests.

You would never notice those individual details, but the aggregate effect puts you into a different world.

Efficient Interactions

Being efficient with customers is another standard of gold service treatment. This doesn't mean you have to be lightning-fast, but every interaction needs to mean something and move the customer along the journey toward your product or service.

You want to make it easy for people to buy and give you money. There's one bill I pay every month to a business services company, and it is arduous. The site is not easy to use and clunky, and they only take certain forms of payment, not AmEx or Discover. It's a bill I pay every month, but their software does not allow you to create an account, so you must enter your information every time you want to make a payment. I would not recommend this company to anyone, but I continue to do business with them because it's something I can't get anywhere else. It definitely isn't very efficient or customer-friendly.

Customer Engagement

Webster's Dictionary defines engagement as to occupy, attract, or involve. In this definition, we are talking about participation in moments, events, and life. To engage is to become involved with whatever is occupying our focus at that moment in time.

To engage our customers is to create a relationship. And in that, we can achieve our 6th Star. Do you want your business to successfully engage customers in a new way? Take responsibility and announce it! Devote the time and effort to making an announcement, and then try to make it stick.

Reliability

When we think of value, one of the most critical and important virtues we attach to it is reliability.

We can all be reliable because it's completely trainable. Improvement and honesty are what we want in the world of CS. We are here to not just be reliable, but to show our customers that we are consistently working on it.

Here are some ways to do just that.

Intentions - Always be sharp and clear with your intentions. Also, be specific and keep them strong. Keep the time, location, and expectation of accountable events and times. There are no questions here. Set your targets so that you can hit them, and then hit them. Remember that you can lower your expectations to an easier goal if needed. Making a mini goal and hitting is the definition of reliable.

It is much better to lower your goals so that you can hit them, than to remain unreliable.

Order - Order is the series of events that need to take place so that anything in this world can be done. Whenever we have something to do, it's virtually impossible to do it in chaos. To be responsible is to know what comes first, second, third, and so on until you're done. Being reliable is about knowing what needs to come first, not just showing up on time.

Customer Follow-Up: The "After-Party"

If you have ever watched an award show or a sports championship on TV, you always hear talk about the "after-party." For many people who are invited to attend these parties, they seem to be more excited for the after-party than they are for the event itself.

Whether it's the Academy Awards, the Super Bowl, the World Series, or the Emmys, special events have some sort of event afterwards that gets people excited to attend. In many cases, it becomes an event all by itself. This is when you see interviews with the movie stars or athletes and get to see them in a relaxed environment with big smiles on their faces.

There's an enthusiasm for "what comes next," and it's built around the concept of the after-party. What if you were able to create the same kind of excitement in your customers so they had high anticipation for what comes next? They can give you some money for some sort of product or service, but that's where the real fun begins!

Your local Chamber of Commerce is a perfect example of this. You decide to pay for your annual membership, and this gives you VIP access to weekly networking meetings, monthly luncheons, business support, advertising assistance, personal coaching/mentoring from other members, and much more. It's all the stuff that comes after your purchase is made.

What if you were able to create a feeling in the mind of your customers that they are now part of an incredibly special VIP club that has all sorts of perks? This is a great project for the back deck and another good cup of coffee!

One of the key words in CS that is often overlooked (not in this book!) is experience. This is the time spent on the other side of our service existence. CX is their lives, hopes, expectations, and needs being met, and so on. When we follow-up with our customers, we improve the overall experience.

After the sale is made, problems have the potential of happening. Products and services can and will break down, so a follow-up can proactively help to solve problems. When we offer help and solve problems before they can occur, we avoid the negative. If you want a practical example of this, consider what a follow-up discussion is worth versus a refund of money or product.

Problems with products happen. Most of the time, it isn't anyone's fault. Nobody likes it when things don't work. A follow-up builds a level of trust, especially if there has been some sort of issue with a product or service. Trust between a customer and company is a tricky tightrope indeed, but it can be strengthened with a follow-up.

Follow-ups also allow our companies to get direct feedback. More often than not, our customers only speak when they want to either praise or condemn. Mediocrity gets little attention. A follow-up can open a dialogue that we normally would not achieve otherwise. The benefit of this dialogue is not just improving ourselves. It is a fact that feedback is essential for product development and improvement.

Feedback also creates the possibility of word of mouth referrals. Our follow-ups can lead to buzz about us that may otherwise be lost. Word of mouth advertising is an immensely powerful tool to have in your company.

We are getting our customers to help themselves at this point again. When a friend or family member recommends our services to someone else because we have a creative, caring follow-up, that may create free sales.

What is more effective to build trust? Advertising, or word of mouth recommendations from family or friends? Both offer a connection to our company. We tend to think that there is more trust in each other than a billboard or commercial.

Most businesses are happy to get a sale and don't think about the after-party.

Play Favorites with Customers

Treating customers like gold creates loyalty that brings people back to you again and again. Gold Star service is critical for initial interactions, but it is equally important for long-term relationships. It is those long-term customers that we often take for granted and forget about.

If lurkers and tire kickers see you interacting with customers in a fun way, they will want to be a part of that experience.

Don't be afraid to praise your favorite customers in public. We laugh about wanted posters in post offices or names of deadbeats on checkout counters, but do we praise and highlight the people we love to interact with?

Do something for long-time customers that they don't expect, the whole white glove treatment. The sky really is the limit here. Brainstorm some ideas on how you can make your long-time customers feel special.

Chapter 4

Star 3: Correct Our Mistakes Quickly & Efficiently

Mistakes happen! That motto is reminiscent of the cruder bumper sticker stuck to many cars years earlier that should be plastered on every wall in our business.

So often, we let mistakes ruin us. It's not the mistakes that hurt, but our response. Rather than admit we haven't attained perfection and ninja-like business skills, we prefer to ignore it or sweep things under the rug.

Our mistakes and failures serve as a warning light that we can better. Sometimes, it is only a small tweak to your processes or a quick response to a customer, but that one tweak can 10X results.

Mistakes are the check engine light of the business. When I was in college, a friend and I decided to drive from Fort Collins, Colorado to Coeur d'Alene, Idaho for the long Thanksgiving weekend to see my family. He had an old Datsun 4-door that had seen better days, but it ran and got great gas mileage.

After about 100 miles, the engine started to make some funny sounds, and then it quit in the middle of the highway. I looked at the dash to see if I could see any lights, but there was nothing... until I looked closer and discovered that the "check engine" light had been covered up with duct tape! I took the tape off, and my friend tapped on the light, hoping it would disappear.

Needless to say, our trip took on a whole new complexion after that. A couple of tow trucks, 2 buses, and a ride from a nice lady in a Rambler later, we finally made it to our destination. All that excitement could have been prevented if the check engine light would have been dealt with before we left for our trip.

The risk of shelling out dollars for a small problem overrode his ability to fix it. Putting tape over the check engine light of your business is only inviting disaster.

Mistakes should be scary. They are signals that something is broken. Once seen in this light, we can rejoice when a customer complains. It is an opportunity to transform your business and become a Gold Star business.

Sources for Complaints

Complaints come from two sources:

Poor Delivery: The customer didn't receive what they wanted. The price was different than advertised. It was broken. It didn't work.

You've been there. Usually, it's just a mistake or a product defect. All you really want is the product or service to be fixed. You are not asking for special treatment or more than you paid for, but you have experienced times where you felt like you had to jump through tremendous hoops and walk through fire to get your problem rectified. It's painful, and you feel like a criminal trying to get something done. This is the experience we want to avoid.

Poor Experience: The customer got what they wanted, but the whole experience was so poor and inefficient that they will find someone else to solve their problems in the future. As a company this is harder to discover and one of the reasons you must poll your customers on a regular basis. Deep down, you thought you gave the customer what they wanted, but you can't understand why they never came back.

It was the experience. You made it difficult and probably didn't respect them. You must provide opportunities for them to tell you about it so you can make changes.

Handling Complaints

Here are a couple of facts about customer complaints. It's commonly accepted that about 1 out of 25 customers will make a complaint to a company. An unhappy customer will tell approximately 15 people about their bad experience, multiplying the problem and hurting your reputation. Scary, very scary.

Be Humble

To be humble or not may be the only way to soften a mistake for a guest or customer. There are times when either or both may be required. You would think that not being humble would make customer relations fail, but some customers see humility as a weakness when they are looking for strength. The skill of the CEA to achieve the 6th Star will require knowing when to be humble and when to show strength.

Showing strength is not as difficult as being humble so let's talk a bit about being humble. How do we cultivate humility?

We start by spending time listening to others. In the world of CS, we are in a position where we are required to listen. This skill can be honed into more than just hearing what our customers have to say. Asking questions is essential to truly listen because our customers may not know how to express their needs. It is up to us to nudge them along and get to their needs. That cannot be accomplished without engagement.

Stay Calm

We all know people can be unreasonable at times, and emotions run high when people feel wronged. It's easy to get dragged into drama, and it's hard not to take attacks on your business personally. You must step back, remain calm, and see this an opportunity to change your customer's outlook. Remaining calm in the face of accusations of mistakes diffuses the situation and allows you to make real progress.

Listen

Don't talk. Don't defend. Don't even offer suggestions. Just listen, ask questions, and understand the why behind their complaint. It may not be what you expect. The worse action you can take is to solve something that is not the real problem.

Acknowledge Your Mistake

Most of us aren't used to hearing people admit to their mistakes. When we do, it can disarm us. That's the same reaction customers often have when you admit something went wrong. It may not have even been a true mistake. The error revealed an error in expectations. Apologizing and telling them thank you creates an awareness of their business and will solve many a problem.

Correct It Quickly

Don't sit on the complaint. The customer rarely forgets, even if the interaction up to this point has been positive. Find a way to make their experience right and do it immediately!

Follow-Up

Follow-up is the extra mile you can take that no one expects. Check back the next day and take a pulse of the customer. This check-in has the potential to create a fan for life.

Be Proactive

How do we avoid a complaint before it even happens? Is there a way to be proactive going about it? Yes, it has been done by servers for hundreds, if not thousands of years.

One of the best ways to describe proactive CS is doing something for your customer before they need it. For example, an excellent 6th Star server will fill a water glass before a customer asks for it. On the customer's side, the glass fills itself without effort, contemplation, or even having to speak out loud.

This is not to say that asking for more water is a complaint. It is to say that getting to what our customers need before they ask is a way to be proactive with potential complaints.

Let's talk about two practical ways to be proactive with our service.

First and foremost, make your company available. Close to half of the companies out there right now have no way of reaching them. If they do, the contact information is not visible to the public. Nearly 50% of all companies feel that it's not important that customers be able to make direct contact with them, which blows me away. No wonder the customer feels like businesses don't care about them.

In today's age, we need to let customers have a channel of their choice. Phone, email, and social media are all ways to make sure our companies can be contacted, and we need to give our customers many ways to contact us as possible.

Second, get your customers to help themselves. It may feel like a weakness if we post what may go wrong with our services or goods. However, a customer can look at that and fix or improve our goods themselves, which has more benefit than just one less customer complaint call. Something as simple as posting a list of FAQs on your website can help your customer education tremendously and lead to fewer issues.

When we get our customers to help themselves and focus on improvement, there is a pride. When we focus on improving our customers, we are proactively getting up and handling complaints before they even happen. This is not magic. It is understanding and examining where parts of our companies can break and putting in a step-by-step guide for when they do. This allows our customer to improve themselves at the same time.

Our company's weaknesses are manifested in their complaints. Customers complain because they want to improve their lives. Getting to them first is a key practice to getting our 6th star. Not being afraid to show weakness is the CS of the future. In showing weakness, we find that a connection between business and customer becomes much stronger.

Am I Handling Complaints Effectively?

* We encourage positive and negative feedback from customers.

* We have a clear complaint handling procedure.

* We respond quickly to complaints regardless of the route and channel used?

* We are polite in responding to complaints.

* We take ownership of complaints.

* We make acknowledge the mistake to the degree it was broadcast.

* We establish the facts of the complaint.

* We record the details of the complaints for resolution and future improvements.

* We create deadlines for resolving complaints.

* We keep customer informed of the progress of their complaint.

* We follow-up with customers after the problem is resolved.

Chapter 5

Star 4: Create An Unparalleled Culture of Customer Service Excellence

Marriott, Hilton, Starbucks, Apple, and Nordstrom are companies that have built their empires around putting the customer at the top of the food chain.

As you are discovering, creating a customer-centric business is much more than a single event or an individual employee. It requires that every fiber of the business corpus be calibrated with that Mason jar of gold in mind. It begins with the vision of ownership and cascades down into every nook and cranny of the business.

Every employee, piece of literature, aspect of the website, and anything else has the chance to come in contact with a customer.

Companies that feel that their success comes from developing better products, creating more robust services, and building a bigger website are completely missing the boat. Having the best product in the universe doesn't matter if you don't take care of your customers first.

The companies that get it right are the ones that are consistently and unabashedly looking at the world through the eyes of their customer. If you can do this, the entire business world will open its arms to you and magical things will begin to happen.

Your sales and service people are the face of your agency. Very few people in your office talk with your customers as much as they do. Whether people continue to do business with you or not is often based on the relationship they establish with your staff. If there is stress in your office, your people are grumpy, or working conditions are miserable, that will be communicated to your customers.

We all know this is true. Think about the times you call your cable or phone company. The monotone, robotic, depressing sounds that come from the receiver tell you that many of those people are miserable. If you could escape from doing business with them, you would.

How about visits to the DMV? Depressing! It's not the customers that drive the misery. It's the people behind the counter. They are bored or discontented and their attitude produces a fog of depression in every corner of the office. It's a perfect example of what can happen when a frontline employee must deal with hundreds of people a day. They can get cranky and burned out rather quickly unless there is special care given to keeping their attitude alive and well.

Not only are service people the face of s business, but they have the power to create and shape the culture of the office.

I see this all the time. My regular trips to XYZ Insurance are tense and unhappy. There are whispers and gossiping, then I walk in the door and attitudes are dramatically changed. There is energy, people are smiling, and the office seems to be having fun! What happened? The customers are the same, the owners are the same, and the office hasn't been redecorated. After putting on my detective hat and asking a few questions, I discovered that "Rosalind" left last week for another job.

One sour soul poisoned the agency culture. Once she left, the attitudes turned on a dime. No one would argue the point that great or bad service people can not only impact customers but infect your whole operation. Attitude is contagious.

Is it enough? I don't think so. It's has become so understood that great service is a baseline. To become great, there is more. Figuring out ways to create customer loyalty and enhancing their experience with you will really set you apart.

Employees as Part of The Customer Experience

A business owner should think of employees as a big part of the overall CX. Engagement in business for employees is changing. Old ways of doing business are withering and dying, and the new breed wants more than just false promises from a company that is going to pull the rug out from under them at the last minute.

Our employees who do service for us are our soldiers. They understand the assignment, are ready to take the risks, and know what the potential is of the public. So, how do we engage them? Can we do it in a new way?

Maybe some of the old ways are the best. If an old way is forgotten and lost and we bring it back, does it become new? I think it does. We are looking for a new spin on an old-fashioned way of engagement.

That is most likely the difference between dealing with our service and business staff. Our service staff cares more about the success of the interaction than the bottom line. If you tell them to stop connecting because time is money, they'll laugh in your face.

Many people who call to connect with the CS department within companies don't realize the pressure that some of the individuals in these call centers are under. They take the calls to "help" the customer achieve satisfaction with whatever problem it is they are experiencing, yet they are under mandates by the company to keep the calls as short as possible and take as many calls as they can within their allotted work schedule. That is the "why" people aren't always getting the CS they deserve or even expect, when they purchase goods or services. Their CEA's are being penalized for spending too much time helping them!

Does extra time spent with a customer equate to the bottom line? Absolutely, it does. Our CEAs must be paid for the time they spend on the phone helping customers. But those are short term numbers. Our thoughts should be more focused on the long-term effect in these instances. Poor CS filled with unresolved issues reflects on the reputation and good standing of our company. That is where an excessive focus on the bottom line can really come back to bite us.

It is also very demoralizing for individuals when they get failure after failure in resolving problems for the people with whom they communicate regularly. To engage our employees in a new way is to create a new place for them to thrive, which in turn allows our company to grow and thrive.

Tools For The Customer Service Team

In the world of CS, employees who face the public must be armed and ready. That may sound a little harsh, but we are talking about the long term. To deny or constrict resources to the front lines is to make it so that CEA's will fail. It's that simple.

Supply the front line or lose.

Delegate With Development In Mind

Those who serve must deal with almost constant changes. That is the daily challenge those of us in CS face every day. It is also what gives us a sense of pride and accomplishment. When we talk about delegation, it is a simple process. There is a chain of command, and messages get passed up and down.

When we allow our representatives to be a part of the development, our service improves. Difficulties may arise because our service staff may be the most creative in the company. Even the advertising/design department does not have to deal directly with the public, only public perception. Creative individuals develop in unique ways, and some of those ways may look on the surface as unorthodox at best, maybe even insane.

If your company is going to offer the empowerment of development, then you may want to try out some interesting concepts. Just keep in mind that some of the greatest success stories in human history were considered madness at the time they were implemented.

Expectations

Expectations for the CS staff should be simple, direct, and short. If the expectations are too demanding or convoluted, it is almost certainly tying the hands of some of the most needed people, preventing them from doing the best they can for the company and its reputation.

Autonomy

The ability to think on our feet during an encounter with a customer is essential for a true connection. When an issue presents itself directly to you, having the ability to make a decision on the spot is not only important to your customer, but to your value as a CEA.

Vision

Your connection to your customers or clients is your most direct vision. We can debate that a room of people looking at the future of sales is vision. However, that is not as direct as what happens down in the trenches. Your true vision will always be how you see your customers, and how they see you.

Recognize Hard Work

This may require more liberties than normal as well. Your CS relations are a much more volatile part of your company than others. This is not to say that your CS staff is the hardest working staff. Many people choose to go into CS because they can apply the skills they excel at.

The difference in recognizing the efforts of someone who is in a service industry and someone who is not is interesting. The pride in keeping a customer who was going to leave is one of the best rewards for a CEA, but how should a company recognize them? We cannot recognize our service staff in the same way as the rest of our employees. Even a slow day for them is hard.

To recognize service is to express love or adoration. In other words, the best way to recognize them is to let them know what they mean to the company over and repeatedly. And remember, the creative admire creativity, so try to come up with new ways of letting them know how much you appreciate them.

The level of creativity needed to deal with the public on a day-to-day basis requires a great deal of effort and energy. So, what are the practical steps we can take to build a culture of engaged people willing to create vibrant CX's?

1. Hire Customer Service Super Stars

Job descriptions should always be customer-focused. Within an organization, you are either serving the customer directly or serving someone who does. Describing everyone's job description in these terms will form the expectation you have from job seekers. You will begin to attract people who can impress customers or have a deep desire to learn these skills.

It will signal to all employees that your company not only cares that great service is paramount, but also mandates a high level of effort. Regardless of what position you are hiring for, you can ask questions during the interview like:

★ What's the nicest thing you've ever done for a customer or someone you didn't know?

★ Describe what exceptional customer service looks like.

★ What do you think the most important part of this job will be?

Even if their answers are not satisfactory, you can identify how they will be with people. In my experience, I can tell within about 2 minutes of starting the interview if the person sitting across the table from me will make it in our company. If they have those soft people skills, I can easily direct them to be more customer-focused and think deeply about how that will impact their job.

In my career, I have probably interviewed well in excess of 3,000 people from all walks of life and have always tried to hire a certain type of person. Many of my companies have been very technical in nature, but I've always felt I could teach someone the skills of the job. It's much more difficult to train an attitude.

I have a friend who owns a very technical business, but he has never hired for skill sets. He feels he can teach someone to be a master technician, but their attitude is something that is buried deep within their DNA and is near impossible to change.

Here's a little inside scoop. He mostly hires food servers and bank tellers because they already have a servants' heart. Most of the time, they turn into amazing employees.

Here's how it works. He pre-interviews people without them even knowing it. Whenever he goes the bank or any local food establishment, he looks for people who absolutely love their customers and go above and beyond the call of duty. He knows they aren't making much in the jobs they have, and he knows he could provide a more stable source of income once they learn the hard skills.

Once he has convinced this person has the CS chops, he offers them a job. It works like a charm, and he always has staff that exceeds other similar businesses.

2. Empower Your People

Ritz Carlton makes every employee carry a customer credo card. This is discussed every day in huddles and debriefs to make sure the company is committed to the principles they believe in.

They give each employee a sizable budget every day per customer to enhance their CS efforts. Your business may not have the budget to deliver this level of service, but there are small ways you can empower your people to make a difference without running back to management every time there is an issue.

Even though Ritz-Carlton has an impressive budget, you can still adopt their service values to empower your people. Look at their 12 service values and see if you get any ideas on how you can raise the bar for you CS:

1. I build strong relationships and create Ritz-Carlton guests for life.

2. I am always responsive to the expressed and unexpressed wishes and needs of our guests.

3. I am empowered to create unique, memorable, and personal experiences for our guests.

4. I understand my role in achieving the Key Success Factors, embracing Community Footprints, and creating The Ritz-Carlton Mystique.

5. I continuously seek opportunities to innovate and improve The Ritz-Carlton experience.

6. I own and immediately resolve guest problems.

7. I create a work environment of teamwork and lateral service so that the needs of our guests and each other are met.

8. I have the opportunity to continuously learn and grow.

9. I am involved in the planning of the work that affects me.

10. I am proud of my professional appearance, language, and behavior.

11. I protect the privacy & security of our guests, my fellow employees, and the company's confidential information and assets.

12. I am responsible for uncompromising levels of cleanliness and creating a safe and accident-free environment.[7]

Give employees latitude and ownership to fix problems and find ways to enhance the CX. Have your people regularly share success stories they have with other customers. You should also try to avoid micromanagement at all costs. If you are a perfectionist, you must allow your people to be different from you. Remember, nobody will do things exactly like you. Some will do it better, some worse, but it will always be different. If you force your people into too small of a box, you will frustrate them. Give them leeway to act, and let their natural abilities dictate how they serve your customers. It will pay off in the long run.

So often, employees want solve problems, but they don't have the tools to make things right. Analyze what employees have and what keeps them from operating effectively, then give them those things!

3. Incentivize Employees To Prioritize Customers

When you hear the word "incentives", you immediately think about extra dollars you can earn for hitting certain benchmarks. It may be cold hard cash, a gift card from the local coffee shop, or getting off an hour early on Friday afternoon. Don't limit yourself to money. Most people are competitive by nature and love a good game. You can create a point system or even team goals that groups can reach for.

Try to think like Harry Potter. In those stories, all the students were divided into houses, and everything they did contributed to points for the whole house. At the end of the year, the points were totaled, and rewards were given to the winning house. Design a system of customer excellence around a team, and your people will compete to create ideas and systems for advancing your customer-centered culture.

You will always have superstars rise to the top in any internal challenge. Some will shine so bright that those behind them will be tempted to give up. There's an easy way to bypass this without frustrating your top and bottom performers. Give incentives to the top people regardless of the team they are on, but also reward the team. This keeps those who feel they can't win an individual award continuing to strive for a reward they will receive as a team.

4. Align Systems and Processes to be Customer-Centered

Are employees set up for success, or do processes and procedures get in the way of providing Gold Star experiences? Do you have processes in place that create extra work and friction for employees? Look for those areas of friction and find ways to remove them. Anything that blocks the ability to service the customer will diminish your ability to generate a pleasant experience.

By removing those hurdles from employee work, you again signal that the customer is the ultimate focus. Sometimes, this can only happen by regularly listening to your employees and gathering feedback on what in their work inhibits them from being the best for the customer.

Nothing frustrates me more than having to shop for a new phone. It's a terrible process. The time I spend in the phone store is always longer than expected, even when I prep myself for the experience. Something is always wrong, and you can even see it on the face of the employees. They have no quick way to solve my problems. Nothing is clear, and I always feel like I am being charged more than necessary. It became so stressful that I now purchase my new phones directly from an app on my phone!

I am sure you can think of examples in your own life as a consumer that frustrate you. Outline those steps, then begin applying them to your own business. Are there areas where you can provide better service, but the systems don't allow it?

5. Establish Charitable Projects Employees Care About

Charity may seem like an odd way to improve customer-focused culture, but nothing shouts to your community that you care about them more than being involved in charitable causes.

Customers, especially millennials, want to do business with companies that are trying to make the world a better place. Customers will fall in love with you for having a mission.

The best place to begin is with your employees. Involve them in this mission. Find organizations they care about that align with the company goals. They will become enthused about promoting within the organization, and this will bleed over into how they care for individual customers who interact every day with your business.

Caring for people multiplies like a virus. If your people can do good for the world, that same spirit will infect them when they interact with your customers.

Culture of Excellence

- ★ Do I have a clear vision for customer service excellence that is distributed throughout my company?

- ★ Do my hiring practices reflect my statement of excellence?

- ★ Does onboarding new employees integrate our standards of excellence?

- ★ Do executives and leadership regularly interact with customers?

- ★ Do we distribute and reward stories of excellence within the company?

- ★ Are our people empowered to make customer service decisions?

- ★ Is compensation linked with customer satisfaction?

- ★ Do we have fun with our customers?

- ★ Do we have a safe, positive employee environment that lends itself to customer service excellence?

* Are our people competent on all products and services?

Chapter 6

Star 5: Build A Relationship Based On Mutual Respect

We all love to be respected and know how important it is. Survey after survey of CS organizations highlight this key fact. The key takeaway in every survey is that almost nothing you do will matter if a customer feels disrespected.

The problem is that respect can be so individual and fuzzy to define. You've seen this in your personal life when you've hurt a relationship unknowingly and offended someone. Then you had to work on repairing the relationship over time.

Being disrespected is a hot button issue for most customers in the world. In a survey by www.customersthatstick.com, 75% of customers said they were not likely to do business with a company if they felt disrespected by an employee of the organization. A full ¾ of people will choose to do business elsewhere if we do not show them respect as a customer. That means that you just alienated most of your potential customers in one fell swoop.

We could argue that people need to grow up and get a thicker skin. People shouldn't be offended so easily, and they just need to deal with it. This may be true in many cases. Sometimes, it feels like we are walking through a minefield, but the sales process is a two-way street. You must give respect to receive it.

There are behaviors you can change and implement to show respect and honor to those you do business with. That's what we are all about, isn't it? It would pay to brush up on your respect skills, so you stand out in a world of offensiveness.

Do you see your customers as a wheel in the machine of your business? Are they just a means to an end? Are they a dollar sign with a face? Worse, are they a necessary evil and a nuisance?

If you think of them this way, respect will never come. If you own a business, you entered the industry because you had a solution to a problem people had. Your ultimate desire was to give value to people and get rightly paid for it. The dollars were just a scorecard demonstrating your ability to solve problems and create value for people, so much value that people were willing to trade their hard-earned cash to get it from you.

You must deeply believe that people are worthy of respect. Sometimes, this can be difficult, and you may need to play some mental gymnastics to get in the right frame of mind. By changing your attitude toward people, you demonstrate your desire to respect people where they are.

Ways to Show Respect

Beyond changing your own attitude and the attitude of your employees about who customers are, there are key social basics we can all practice to creating a more respectful environment for our customers.

Most of us know the basics. Say "please" and "thank-you", make eye contact, and listen with intent. If you've ever been to Chick-Fil-A, the employees are drilled to use "my pleasure" every time a customer says, "thank you." Same with Marriott. It displays a level of respect you don't get from most other businesses. You come away feeling like they enjoyed your business and hope you come back. Maybe it's a little hokey Southern hospitality, but it works, and at least they aren't saying "Come back now, ya hear."

Whether you have an online business or a brick and mortar operation, nothing shows disrespect more than when you make yourself inaccessible to customers. Many online businesses are so tempted to hide behind the digital screen and make every effort for customers to jump through a million prompts and hurdles to get a question answered.

Online businesses that do well make contact information accessible. Live chats have solved much of this problem, and current technology has made this much easier to navigate. I use it myself by default when I have a question. I know I could search through multiple FAQs and find the answer myself but communicating with a human or advanced AI is so much more convenient.

For the brick and mortar store, the firewall is the manager. When problems or questions arise, we rarely empower our people to respond adequately, but defer to the invisible manager. This may be necessary, but often delays problem solving and disrespects the time of the customer.

An easy solution is to compile the list of common problems customers tend to have and give your people the power to solve those issues. No doubt there will be times when a service issue needs to be escalated, but these should be 10-20% of the issues and not the majority.

We've seen a recent change in car buying due to innovative companies like Carvana. They use this accessibility issue like a wedge in their advertising against traditional car sales. Rather than negotiating with a salesperson only to be told "I need to speak with the manager," you get to deal directly with the person you are buying the car from. This advertising works because accessibility is such a big component of showing respect to the customer.

By virtue of having a business, you make an unspoken promise. "You will have a problem solved via my product or service." Not solving those problems shows deep disrespect.

To solve this potential obstacle, put the promise you offer customers into concrete terms where customers can see it and employees can embody it. Be proud of it, take ownership of it, and by all means let the world know about your promises.

Keep your promise front and center in the minds of your customers, and people will further your ability to meet those promises.

GEICO's ubiquitous promise of "15 minutes or less can save you 15% or more on car insurance." Can they really save every customer on their car insurance? Probably not, but they can keep that 15-minute promise. It's measurable and effective. Everyone is willing to give up 15 minutes to save money. The company can measure how long it takes for an online agent to generate a quote. They keep that promise, and it's one of the reasons they continue to be a dominant player in their industry.

Starbucks is another big brand with a big promise: "To inspire and nurture the human spirit – one person, one cup and one neighborhood at a time." If you have visited one of their stores, and I know you have, you know they keep this promise. The layout of the store reflects this promise. It is comfortable, you never feel rushed, and you almost feel at home. The design invites a neighborhood feeling.

The baristas at the counter communicate this in their interaction with you. You feel good about spending too much on a caffeinated beverage in their stores. It's what keeps people coming back to Starbucks time and time again. Many coffee shops have this same vibe when you walk in and it makes you feel valued.

Everyone wants to be treated like a special person, but we often feel like a number or just another faceless customer. Companies that make us feel special are rare indeed.

Not long ago, I walked into a local business just to browse. I needed to waste some time while one of the kids was at a sports practice. As I browsed through the store, I noticed one employee greeting many of the customers by name. He didn't have to do that. It was apparent that many of these customers were regulars, but the power of using those people's names impressed me so much. It made me feel special, even though no one in the store knew my name!

You can't know all your customers, but I've seen banks and supermarkets use the same trick to perfection. As soon as they see your name on your debit card or in your file, they begin using it. This completely changes the transaction and makes things personal.

I love going to the Tex-Mex chain Moe's. I love the quick and somewhat healthy food options, but I love the greeting everyone gets when they walk in the door. The counter is always watching, and as someone walks in one or more employees shouts out,

"Welcome to Moe's". You instantly smile even if you were expecting it.

If you have customer data, there's a good chance you have birthdays in your database. Use this as an opportunity to celebrate the person and look for ways to connect on a personal level.

Treating others like you would like to be treated is a great starting point, but It may not go far enough if you want to stand out among your competitors. Dave Kerpen developed what he calls the Platinum Rule: "Do unto others as they would want done to them."

The uniqueness of the respect you show will ultimately be defined by your customer target. Once again, this goes back to knowing your customers and those you want to reach. You are not reaching everyone, and you should know your customer targets better than your competitors. Knowing this will allow you to tailor your respect approach differently.

Show Empathy

When we share, we find what each other is going through. How we get to a customer's needs addresses the sharing side of empathy in business, which means that CEA's will have to feel what all the customers feel.

Imagine feeling a hundred or more waves of anger, disappointment, or disgust per day. Then, put in a forty-plus hour workweek of sharing those feelings every day. It must be done to achieve the 6th Star. There is no way around it. Someone working in the CS field will never achieve extra credit without empathy.

So, how do we get to a place where those who are dealing with all these negative emotions survive their career? We introduce the volume of sharing.

Imagine an old school radio with turn knobs. One knob controls the station. The other knob turns the volume up and down.

We begin by tuning our radios to the emotions of our customers. Once we get to a place where we can hear them clearly, we reach over and turn down the volume. This is not showing disrespect to our customers. We must remember that empathy is a two-way street. More likely than not, our customers have no intention of understanding the emotions of our employees.

The connection IS the sharing. When we are with those we trust, we can share as loud as we want. However, we are going to turn down the volume with our clients so that our employees can maintain a career with us and still retain their sanity. Often when you are dealing with those who are gifted in the art of empathy, the volume control is not always properly used. This means that training in this art will have to take place with our staff. Some think of this as diffusing. We do not want to diffuse our customers. It is our purpose to lower the volume so that the CEA can do their job.

This is a sadness that leaves those attempting to achieve the 6th Star at a true loss. We must train empathy. It must be in our meetings, on our Zoom calls, and on the front lines.

Many other solutions to respect have been discussed in previous chapters, such as owning up to your mistakes quickly, then solving the problem. Learning and perfecting those skills of listening, apologizing, and responding quickly to customer issues will boost respect in the eyes of your customers.

Relationships Built On Respect

* Do we value our customer's time?
* Do we treat customers like individuals by knowing their history and using their names?
* Do we stay positive and keep a helpful attitude when interacting with customers?
* Do we exceed customer experience metrics we have in place?
* Do we have loyalty programs for customers?
* Do we have referral programs for customers?
* Do we show regular appreciation for our customers?

Chapter 7

Star 6: Never Forget That Customers Are The Most Important Part Of Our Business

I have a process that I go through every time I decide to develop a new product, launch a new business, or build a new brand. I call it "popcorning," and it's something I've done for most of my entrepreneurial career.

It's the process of putting the main concept down on paper (or on a dry erase board in my office), then brainstorming as many ideas as I can about:

- ★ Who's it for?
- ★ What problem does it solve?
- ★ How it will be packaged?
- ★ Is it a physical product or digital?
- ★ How it will be marketed?

* Who are the competitors?

* What kind of irresistible offer can I create to motivate people to buy?

* How it will be distributed?

* How much of my time will be required to get it to critical mass?

These brainstorms are then shared with my wife, Tami, and other business-minded people for feedback. Typically, she will simply just shake her head when I start a sentence with "Babe, I have an idea." It been a running joke between us for over 20 years.

This same process takes place all over the world whenever someone has an idea for a new product, service, or business. A single person, a team, or an entire organization can "popcorn" their way to the new idea.

There are a few other questions that need to be asked at the very beginning of this process that will make a tremendous difference for your customers:

- ★ What obstacles will customers encounter in deciding to make a purchase?
- ★ How can each of those obstacles be removed?
- ★ Are there any friction points that may hinder their decision to purchase?
- ★ What is our game plan for follow up with each customer once they have made the purchase?
- ★ What will we do to get the customer to come back to us a 2nd time?
- ★ Do we have a plan to incorporate customer feedback into our loop? What is it?

There are many other questions you can ask yourself, but this will at least get your creative juices flowing in the right direction.

Bottom line. You must get into the habit of looking at your business from the customer's viewpoint, not yours. Don't get hung up on profits or number of units sold. Focus on ways to enhance the CX at every turn, and the profits will follow.

You love your business and the services and products you deliver to customers. Without customers, all your systems, processes, and wonderful products do not matter. Ultimately, business is about solving problems for people. It's easy to lose sight of that as we easily become enamored with our own stuff. And yes, you should be excited about and constantly striving for better products, but don't lose sight of the end user.

You must never forget that the customer is the most important part of the business.

This is a tough nugget of truth to swallow. Every decision, process, and system should be crafted with the CX in mind. Without customers, there is no business. Without loyal customers, there is no business longevity.

Customers today are living in a time where trust in institutions is at an all-time low. They are looking for authenticity, originality, honesty, and good intent. When you can communicate these qualities and your business is structured around the needs of people, you will never have an end to people wanting your product.

But business has become democratized. Because of the internet and social media, customers have information at their fingertips. They can do hours of research on you and their problem before they visit your store or site. Customers are used to social media being listening outposts for companies to tailor their products to new needs.

No longer do businesses create products for customers. Customers transform products and services by the way they use them. They have become co-creators, not merely consumers. Knowing this makes crafting a business around them even more important than ever before.

Old Definition Of A Customer

In the recent past, the customer was the person you had direct contact with. For many businesses, this made sense. You knew the person using your product or service. Eventually, many businesses sold to people who distributed their products and lost sight of the end user. Yes, the distributor is considered a customer as well, but it's not the same as having direct contact with the end user. It makes it much more difficult to reach that 6th Star if we don't have a direct dialog with the consumer. If they are dissatisfied, you degrade your ability to provide CS that wins.

Making Customers The Center Of Your Business

If you implement a customer-centric strategy in your business, you will immediately be light years ahead of most of your competitors. The CMO Council conducted a recent survey of Chief Marketing Officers, and only 14% said customer centricity was a hallmark of their company. They also agreed that only 11% of their customers would think of them as customer focused.

So, how do you begin to put customers first and at the center of everything you do?[8]

1. Track Customer-Focused Metrics

Begin putting numbers to customer lifetime value. If you keep a customer engaged and coming back to you again and again, this number can add up rather quickly. How much are they worth over 1 year, 2 years, 5 years, or 10+ years? Having these numbers in mind makes it much easier to spend and allocate resources to creating rich and rewarding CXs.

It will always cost more to acquire new customers versus keeping current ones happy. You can also understand and use the "Net Promote Score." The NPS measures customer loyalty over time by measuring how willing a customer is to recommend your brand to others. Nothing is more telling about customer satisfaction than whether they are willing to promote you to friends, families, and colleagues.

Implementing NPS in your business is not as difficult as you may think. You don't need crazy analytics, large spreadsheets, or fancy surveys to find your biggest fans. There's a good chance you've participated in an NPS survey before and never realized it. In fact, you only need to ask your customer 2 simple questions.

1. How likely are you to recommend our product or service to a friend? Most businesses using NPS do this on a scale of 1 to 10.

2. What is the reason behind the score?

By using a number scale, you can separate your customers into promoters, passives, and detractors. Promoters are those who give you a 9 or a

10. Passives will rate you a 7 or an 8. Detractors will give you a 0 through 6.

You can then calculate your score by subtracting the percentage of detractors from the percentage of promoters. The score will be anywhere from -100 to +100. Having a positive score means that you are on the right track. Analytic companies that track these scores for large companies agree that anything about a +50 shows you are doing above average.

Where's the real power of the score? It's in the feedback you are getting in question 2. You will often find that your detractors give you much more feedback than your promoters. This is a good thing. It will help you identify where you are not meeting needs of clients and give you the opportunity to begin reshaping your business around the customer.

It is a simple analytical tool that helps your business identify the areas where it can exceed expectations and truly make the customer the center of your universe.

2. See Customers As The Solution To Your Goals

Customer feedback is an analytical tool that can help you grow your business. Sometimes, you are so deep in your business that you can't see the forest through the trees. Customers can help you do that. We've talked about understanding and knowing your customers, especially the new ones. It is equally important to creating loyalty while growing your brand.

There are several ways you can do this.

- Provide live chat support.
- Deliver customer satisfaction surveys and incentivize your customers to be honest and provide deep answers to these questions.
- Provide feedback forms at every point of customer contact.
- Use social media to gather information about how people feel about you.
- Use email to gather information via questionnaires.

* Let them know the purpose is to make their experience better, and they will give you plenty to use.

3. Obsess Over Your Customers Instead Of Competitors

Any business should keep a close watch on their competitors. Knowing your competitors and what they offer and how they interact with customers can push you to be better. It's a hallmark of free market capitalism that uses the competitive spirit to push us all toward innovation and excellence.

While you should monitor what your competition is doing, you shouldn't do so at the expense of a more important target: your customers. Obsessing over who they are and what they want is of the utmost importance. By focusing on them more than your competitors, you will reach a level of customer satisfaction that is beyond what your competition is doing.

When you focus on your competitors, you tend to see your flaws and shortcomings in relation to what other businesses are doing. Sometimes, those differences are what make you unique, and your customers love you. Changing those in the face of competitive peer pressure might just hurt your relationship with your customers and damage why they love doing business with you.

If you've never been to the grocery chain, Trader Joe's, you have missed a treat. Before you go, you need to prep yourself. Spend some time online reading customer reviews about Trader Joe's. You'll be amazed at all the love their customers heap on the grocery chain.

Here's an example of such a review from Consumer Affairs:

I shop at the Trader Joe's market in my area nearly every morning. The moment I walk in the store, my mood elevates with the great music they play as well as being greeted by their great crew members. They introduce new items weekly and the prices are right. Their products have no GMOs and there is wide variety of organic dairy, produce and grocery. The wine department is well stocked with an array of different blends at very competitive prices. There is a sample station with featured food of the day and free coffee sample. They also sell household goods and skin care. Trader Joe's is my one stop shop!

Writer Joseph Cohen even penned a book extolling the obsessive customer behavior Trader Joe's creates, called *'Trader Joe's, Take Me I'm Yours!'*

Even one of the book reviews is equally humorous about the love affair customers have:

I love Trader Joe's. You could say I'm addicted to TJ's. So, what a nice surprise to discover Trader Joe's, Take Me I'm Yours! It's really funny. The pictures are a riot. But behind the laughs is a book that totally rings true. I found myself saying again and again "Hey, that's me." It's a book that speaks for every TJ fan. I wish I wrote it!

But you are in for a disappointment the first time you drive up to a TJ's. Many of the stores are old and seem outdated. When you walk in, it is much smaller than your normal supermarket. It feels like an upgraded hippy health food store.

If you stay long enough, though, you will be converted. Employees (or crew members) wear Hawaiian shirts and are willing to greet you and spend all the time you need to be helped. Prices are amazing, and the quality is out of this world. The setup is so comfortable, you will find yourself coming back again and again.

The one thing they do right is being obsessed with customers and not their competitors, and this shows in the way they treat you from the moment you enter the door until the second you leave. Even during the recent pandemic, our local TJ's had long lines of committed customers waiting to get in. They couldn't stay away even when the wait was inconvenient to them.

4. Spy on Your Customers

Sometimes, it can be hard to gather customer data, especially when you are new. There's a secret trick you can use whether you are an online business or brick and mortar store. You can use all the information on the Internet to your advantage.

There is nothing you can think of that doesn't have a forum online. Search for forums that represent your target market. This could be foodies, car enthusiasts, pet lovers, tomato farmers, construction companies, etc. You can find them all.

Lurk among those forums, and you will find what they like and don't like very quickly. Don't be shy either. Participate in the forums and ask questions. If a person is on a forum, they are passionate and aren't afraid to tell you about it. These are the customers you want to listen to.

Amazon is a perfect search engine for customer feedback as well. Find books and products related to your niche, and you'll soon discover in the reviews what people like and don't like. Even for this book, I spent time on Amazon looking at other CS titles. Do you know what I discovered? People strongly dislike theoretical books and are frustrated there is not more practical advice they can immediately apply to their business. This is why I have spent so much ink on practical tips so you can be a 6-Star business!

Social Media is the other outlet for customer information. Facebook has groups devoted to everything as well, and they are no less passionate than forum users. Search, engage, and you will be rewarded.

The last place I would recommend you checking out is Quora. This is an online site dedicated to answering questions people have. You can find multiple questions people ask about your own products and service that will give you insight. The other benefit is that you can easily create an account and start answering questions. You quickly can become an expert that people will flock to have their own problems solved. This is smart marketing and has been used by many businesses to create traffic and loyalty.

5. Sweat The Small Stuff

Nothing is more frustrating for a business owner than for a customer to monopolize your time only to purchase something small and insignificant that does not come close to paying for the time you spent with them.

But these customers are perfect case studies in creating loyalty and customer awareness. Turn those customers into raving fans by following up with them and creating a deeper need. People don't expect this. Why would a company reach out when a person only purchased something so small? These exchanges can help you develop loyalty and WOW people into coming back for more.

6. Make Customers Part Of The Customer Service Process

Customers are often left out of the process. We as companies do this to protect ourselves. As customers, we accept this because sometimes we simply want a service given to us as without knowing how it is done. That man behind the curtain, ignore him, please.

The process of CS is in the interaction between the buyer and seller. To include the buyer in the process of CS is to assign importance to the event of the purchase itself. When money is exchanged, service begins. This is the difference between a CEA and someone who is serving you dinner in a restaurant. In the restaurant, money is not exchanged until the end of the meal. Imagine how the staff would react if you gave your gratuity upfront.

When we include our guests, buyers, and customers in the process, we may want to consider a limited approach. There is often no approach at all, so even a little inclusion can yield a great result. Begin small at first and build your way up to a comfort level that works for you.

The 'why' for inclusion is so that your customers will have more options. A single road is not service. Service–true service–is flexible. When we limit our guests to a single road without signs or indicators, we offer them nothing but a single option.

The most brilliant of CS will be to include options for our customers within our service. If you are curious about how this could apply to the needs of your own company, try this...

Talk to your customers—live. Do not survey them. Take time and actually talk to them! They will eventually tell you what you need to do to include them. Then, implement that... and that 6th Star will magically appear.

We know from experience that the more you allow the customers access to you, the more involved they will become. Involving them in your process means you never forget the customer is the most important part of your business.

Chapter 8

The Good, The Great, And The Terrible

Sometimes, the best way to get a grasp onto the 6th Star service is to see it in action. I want you to come away from this book with clear actionable items that can change your business and life. Theory is great, but most of us need to see skin on it to really grasp the concept. We also learn through contrast, so not only do I want to show you the best 6-Star service in action, but also display some of the worst. If nothing else, the worst will be a bit of comic relief as you cultivate your strategy inside your business.

Zappos

One of the customer service superstars is online shoe seller, Zappos. We've talked about them already. Their CEO made a commitment from the beginning of the company to have a religious-like dedication to the customer experience. If you search online for Zappos customer service stories, you will find hundreds of examples and glowing reviews from customers.

However, this particular story from December 2012 set the record for being the longest customer support call ever, lasting 10 hours and 29 minutes. Talk about dedication. Nobody really knows what they discussed, that has been kept private. Apparently, the person needed someone, and the Zappos employee was there to be that sounding board. It did result in a sale, but the world record phone may have been more impressive.[9]

Sainsbury

Sainsbury is the UK's equivalent of Wal-Mart or Target. You can find anything there from groceries to clothing to general home supplies. Inside of their bakery, they sell a bread called Tiger Bread. It has a mottled brown and white appearance because of the way it bakes. A young customer, 3-year-old Lily Robinson, wrote a letter to Sainsbury asking: *"Why is tiger bread called tiger bread? It should be called giraffe bread. Love from Lily Robinson, age 3 and 1/2."* To be honest, if you see the bread, Lily is right. It looks much more like the pattern on a giraffe than a tiger.

The store didn't ignore this small customer service question. Chris King, a customer service staff, replied: *I think renaming tiger bread giraffe bread is a brilliant idea—it looks much more like the blotches on a giraffe than the stripes on a tiger, doesn't it?*

He did explain, *It's called tiger bread because the first baker who made it a looong time ago thought it looked stripey like a tiger. Maybe they were a bit silly.* He also included a gift card and signed the letter, *Chris King, age 27 and 1/3.* Lily's mother blogged about the story, and it went viral. Sainsbury responded once more by renaming the item giraffe bread in honor of little Lily.[10]

Morton's Steak House

Morton's Steakhouse in Hackensack, NJ shows how important it is to continually monitor customer feedback. Like many businesses, Morton's has used social media to hear when their name is being mentioned.

Thankfully, someone very attentive to customer service was manning the station on one faithful night. One customer, Peter Shankman, was on a late night flight to Newark when he tweeted, *Hey @mortons, can you meet me at Newark Airport with a porterhouse when I land in two hours? K, thanks.*

To his surprise, a tuxedo-clad Morton's Hackensack representative was there holding a paper bag with porterhouse steak, colossal shrimp, side potatoes, and bread when he landed. You can imagine the shock on Shankman's face. He was only joking when he fired off the tweet. The logistics of his request were near impossible, and he never expected such service. The person who first saw the tweet had to act, the manager had to sign off on the idea, the chef had to cook the meal, and then a driver had to make the long trek to deliver the bag-o-food. Not an easy task by any stretch of the imagination!

Morton's managed a customer service miracle, and the story peppered social media feeds for weeks.[11]

Lego

11-year-old James Groccia saved his money for 2 years to buy the Lego Emerald Night Train set. When he was ready to make his purchase, the toy had been discontinued. Extremely upset and disappointed, James wrote a letter to Lego expressing his frustration. He received the typical boiler-plate corporate apology letter. Hey, at least they didn't ignore him.

That wasn't the end of the story. A few days before his birthday, a package arrived with the train set and a personal letter from Lego. James' parents caught the birthday surprise on video and shared online. You can bet it went viral, and Lego looked like a hero to block-builders worldwide.[12]

Pearson's Candy

Pearson's Candy is a regional US candy company based in St. Paul, Minnesota. Their customer service story could easily fit into good and ugly customer service buckets. It was their recovery that makes this such a good story.

Fourteen-year-old Dave Bell loved Pearson's salted nut roll. One day after school, he purchased the candy bar, but something wasn't right. It didn't taste like the normal sweet and salty treat he adored. His disappointment motivated him to pick up pen and paper and write a letter of complaint to the company. Deep down, he hoped for a free candy bar in return.

All he got was a standard letter of apology. Now, that's not terrible. Many companies ignore such complaints, especially when they come from a child with little disposable income. However, that's not the end of the story.

Sixty years later, Dave Bell was cleaning his house and discovered this apology letter from Pearson's. The whole incident made him smile, and he decided to email the company and tell the story once more.

This time, Pearson responded differently. They sent Dave a package of several candy bars, including a 5-pound salted nut roll. Pearson's CEO Michael Keller said, "His claim was totally legitimate, and we decided to send him a little bit of free product to make good on what we missed 61 years ago."[13]

Chewy.com

Chewy.com has a reputation for great service and affordable pet products. Benyamin Cohen ordered product from Chewy.com with no complaints about the service, but one package delivery surprised him. He opened the box of dog food, and there was a handwritten note from a Chewy employee. The note thanked him for his order and asked his dog (which they named) to enjoy the food.

No one gets handwritten notes anymore, and this small step surprised him and led him to share his story online. He commented, *In 2013, to receive a handwritten thank you note from a national company really just blew me away.*[14]

Bungie Studios

Bungie Studios is a game development company with titles you may recognize like Destiny and Halo. They are also well known for having one of the best customer service teams in the business.

During one Christmas seasons, one father was worried about his son, who had an upcoming liver transplant service scheduled. Bungie's newest Halo game was supposed to launch during his surgery. The dad sent Bungie a request to do something special for his son. Bungie went above and beyond in their response. They sent a signed get-well card to the boy, a custom helmet based on one of the main characters in the game, shirts, toys, and some custom art pieces from the game's designers. Pretty amazing.[15]

Kroger

Kroger is a grocery chain in the United States based out of Cincinnati, Ohio. This story came out of one of their locations in Suwanee, GA.

One day, a mother and her daughter were in line at the store pharmacy. A pharmacist overhead their conversation. The little girl was about to get a new bed and her own room but was scared about sleeping in the room by herself. Mom was trying her best to give her a pep talk and convince her that there was nothing scary about the room.

The pharmacist quickly put together a spray bottle of water and placed a pharmacy label on the bottle. The prescription was for Monster Spray. She directed the little girl to spray in the room once a day, and no monsters would ever crawl out from under the bed.

The mother was relieved by the generosity of the pharmacist, and the little girl left with confidence. Of course, the mother took the story to Facebook, where she thanked Kroger and the creative pharmacist.[16]

Delta Airlines

Delta Airlines reacted similarly with a recent row they had with Ann Coulter. All of us who have flown understand the diminished service we receive from airlines, so it is easy to want to pile on this industry when someone famous expresses our own pain and frustration.

Coulter spent two days lambasting Delta on Twitter for switching her seat due to a system glitch. She had pre-booked a window seat in the emergency exit row for a $30 upcharge. Most of us love that emergency aisle. Even for short people, the extra leg room almost feels like first class.

Coulter got on the plane and discovered her seat had been changed. She graciously complied with the new arrangement on the plane, but once she had left the flight, she went full force into a Twitter tirade for being switched to a *less desirable seat without explanation, apology, etc.*

The tirade continued, and it was not friendly. She even insulted some of her fellow passengers.

So why is our middle and working class suffering? NOT ROBOTS! Globalism and mass immigration. Immigrants take American jobs (and seats on @Delta).

Hey @Delta, if it was so important for the dachshund-legged woman to take my seat, she should have BOOKED THE SEAT IN ADVANCE. Like I did.

Delta responded: *@AnnCoulter Additionally, your insults about our other customers and employees are unacceptable and unnecessary.*

Then, they offered to refund the extra $30 she paid.

This wasn't enough for Ms. Coulter. Delta responded once more:

We are sorry that the customer did not receive the seat she reserved and paid for. More importantly, we are disappointed that the customer has chosen to publicly attack our employees and other customers by posting derogatory and slanderous comments and photos in social media. Her actions are unnecessary and unacceptable. Each of our employees is charged with treating each other as well as our customers with dignity and respect. And we hold each other accountable when that does not happen.

Delta expects mutual civility throughout the entire travel experience.

We will refund Ms. Coulter's $30 for the preferred seat on the exit row that she purchased.

This was a tough one. Delta didn't seem to be able to resolve her complaint, so the company stood its ground, refunded the money, and defended their employees and other customers. By remaining calm and using clear tones and logic with Ann Coulter, they reinforced their own values of civility and customer commitment.

Even though it may not feel like an immediate win for Delta, responses on Twitter showed pride in Delta that they handled the incident with grace. They may have lost one customer but won many others over in the process.

If I would have been in charge at Delta at the time, the only thing I would have done differently is to also give Ms. Coulter a travel voucher for the inconvenience of the computer glitch. Remember, always be thinking about how you can go above and beyond what the expectation is and try your best to diffuse a stressful situation as quickly as possible. The choice to take the grievance to social media made it difficult for Delta to get a win-win out of the situation, but they did their best.[17]

Valve Software

Valve is another famous game designer. They are led by Gabe Newell, famously known as one of the most creative CEOs in the country and extremely responsive to customers. This story comes from a customer who reach out to ask Gabe for an autograph right before his birthday.

A week later, he got an email saying that Valve was sending him a package and gave him a tracking number. The customer was desperate to discover what was in the surprise package, so he checked online and learn that the package weighed close to 4 pounds.

Here's what he had to say: "I used the tracking number he provided and found that the package weighed close to 4 pounds. I was so excited. Finally, it's two days before my birthday. The package has come in the mail. I opened it up to find not only a Portal mouse pad signed by the Gaben himself, but a copy of the book The Sacrifice with a ton of signatures from Valve employees. Needless to say, it made my life."[18]

Aldi

Aldi is a European-based supermarket that has made inroads in the United States. They are everywhere throughout Europe. Recently, Aldi UK responded to a customer complaint with such grace and poise that it became a perfect example of how a business should respond to problems that threaten to damage their reputation.

An Aldi customer in the UK was frustrated with a product they bought at one of their stores and proceeded to announce their discontent on Facebook. The customer discovered that one biscuit (cookie for

Americans) was missing its chocolate coating in a packet of biscuits.

Most companies would see this as a small infraction. Aldi didn't.

The customer proudly announced on FB: *I have a complaint that I wish to make...I could not believe my eyes. Never in all my life had I seen such a biscuit predicament. What did I do next? Well first, I considered eating it, but then I decided against it because let's be honest, a plain digestive biscuit will never tantalize the taste buds...so having ruined my morning cuppa, I do eagerly anticipate your response.*

Of course, they attached the comment to their page with a picture of the naked digestive biscuit. Oh, the horror!

Aldi's customer service team saw the post (because they are listening to customers) and responded with humor: *The plain digestive is not something to be shunned but celebrated. Look at it, sitting there in plain sight - not having to hide behind its chocolate friend.*

The comment led to a stream of playful banter with the customer and Aldi providing an offline solution. They delivered a new packet of biscuits directly to their front door and threw in a free bag of sugar.[19]

Whirlpool

I personally love Whirlpool products and have had great success with them. Thankfully, they have held up so well for me that I have never had to go through a customer service experience with them. After reading this, you will hope so as well.

In New York City, one of the papers has a column by a gentleman calling himself the Haggler. It's his job to help people when they run into roadblocks with companies. One NYC resident had a problem with her Whirlpool microwave and was getting no help from the company, so she wrote in to the Haggler.

The customer had a Whirlpool technician come to her house 5 times to fix her microwave. The serviceman had replaced 4 parts of the microwave within six months of her original purchase. On this last repair visit, he told her he needed to replace some of those parts again.

At this point, the customer contacted Whirlpool for a replacement microwave rather than another repair that probably wouldn't fix the problem. No one at Whirlpool would listen. In fact, they told her to wait until the 1 year warranty expired, and even then, they would need to send another technician and then wait 6 months to consider whether to exchange it.

Frustrated, she reached out to the Haggler and it got worse. The Haggler contacted Whirlpool on her behalf, and Whirlpool offered a refund under 2 conditions.

1. The customer would have to pay Whirlpool $75 to dispose of the broken machine.

2. She would need to sign a confidentiality clause.

Of course, this wasn't acceptable, and the Haggler ended up writing up the whole scenario in one of the nation's largest newspaper. It obviously didn't help Whirlpool's reputation, and apparently there was no resolution for the customer.[20]

Auto Performance Shop

This story comes out of Orlando, FL. Vince Hansen had taken his Audi S4 into the shop for repairs. A little while later, the repair shop called him and told him that the car was ready. When Vince arrived, the technician took the car out for one more test drive to verify the repairs. While the tech was gone, a phone call came in that he had crashed into another car while making an illegal U-turn. Oops!

No problem. The repair shop had insurance, so they turned in the claim and repaired the customer's car, right?

That's not what happened. The shop owner explained that Mr. Hansen had signed a release when he originally delivered the vehicle releasing the store from any liability of damages. All damages were Mr. Hansen's responsibility. Frustrated but knowing he had insurance. Hansen turned the claim into his carrier knowing they would subrogate the damages back to the repair shop. He discovered that the shop was uncooperative in providing their insurance information.

At this point, Hansen went to his local news station, where the incident about the repair shop was made public. At that point, Hansen's car was repaired, but it is unknown whether damages were ever recovered from the body shop.[21]

I think I've made you squirm enough for one day! You probably have your own horror stories to tell, but these stories are easy to see where things can go right or wrong. What can you do to be one of those companies that excel?

Chapter 9

Where Do We Go From Here?

When kids are little, you can tell them just about anything, and they'll believe you. Sasquatch lives in the forest behind your house; eating your carrots makes you see through walls; your parents are the smartest people in the world. Of course, this truism shatters when they turn twelve and discover that they know everything!

Every parent has lists of "stretched truths" they tell their children. They serve as comical relief in an otherwise treacherous job of raising little humans who will someday rule the world.

When my oldest daughter, Jaycee, was about three, I jokingly told her that I was seven. To a youngster who doesn't have a grasp of concepts like time or age, this is a huge number that's very believable. She didn't know anyone who was that old since it wasn't a subject that regularly came up. I would occasionally remind her during the year I was seven, and it became part of our virtual reality as a family.

Well, my next birthday came, and I turned eight. The next year, I turned nine. By that time, Jaycee began learning about things that were tied to being a certain age, such as TV show ratings, driving privileges, and alcohol consumption. We would sit down to watch a movie on Friday Night Family Date Night. If the movie was PG or PG-13, she'd say, "Daddy, we can't watch this movie because you aren't old enough."

To keep my cover, I'd look at my wife, and begrudgingly find a different movie for my age range. As for driving and alcohol, I said, "They gave me a special license to drive, and you're allowed to drink if you're 150 pounds." This worked. I was able to squeeze more time out of my gig.

When I turned twelve, my house of cards came crashing down.

One day, Jaycee and I drove to the store alone. "Daddy, do you know what's really weird?" she said. "You're twelve. I have classmates with brothers and sisters who are twelve. You're a lot bigger than them. That's really weird!"

My brain began to figure out a creative way to get out of this bind. Something ingenious to tell my grandkids later, that smacked of pure joy.

I looked back at her with a completely straight face, crafting the perfect comeback that was going to change the future of fatherhood forever. She looked at me with her curious, confused eyes waiting for me to speak. And then...

I had nothing. Nothing at all.

"Honey, Daddy has a secret to tell you, but you have to promise not to tell your brother," I said. "I'm not twelve."

Her face turned to complete and utter confusion as she tried to ponder what that meant. I'd just shattered one of her deepest belief systems, and she didn't know how to deal with it. I felt closer to her at that moment than I had ever in her entire life because I was about to tell her one of my deepest, darkest secrets.

"Daddy isn't twelve," I continued. "He's fifty-two."

Total silence. More silence. Followed by even more deadening silence. I knew she was trying to think if she knew anyone that old in her mind. The pin-drop moment lasted for what seemed like an eternity. She spoke words I'll never forget for the rest of my life.

“Does Mommy know you aren’t twelve?” she asked.

“I don’t know, baby girl, but let’s keep it a secret just between us, okay?” I replied, barely keeping it together. “You also have to promise me you won’t tell your brother either, since he doesn’t know yet.”

Every time the family hung out and the subject of birthdays or age came up, we’d look at each other and exchange small winks, then go back to what we were doing. This continued for a few weeks.

One day, Jaycee just had to know if Mommy knew my true age.

“Do you know Daddy isn’t twelve?” she whispered.

My wife, Tami, looked at her and nodded. From then on, this special one-of-a-kind Daddy-Daughter moment was officially over. Within the next year, my son made the same realization, and we had a similar bonding moment when he discovered my real age.

Now, I have a 6-year-old daughter who thinks I’m 12 (I started the same game when she was about

3!) I can tell you one thing for sure. I will enjoy every moment until the magic melts away.

Precious moments such as these can recalibrate our perspectives on how we live our life and treat other people. I don't want to miss a single magical moment with my kids, my friends, or my customers.

It took me many years to arrive at my mind-boggling epiphanies that caused me to reinvent the way my businesses are built from the ground up. I used to be that guy who would put in 80 hours at the office to attain "The American Dream," but now my definition has morphed into something completely different. It's all about having the proper perspective in life and in business.

Now that we have come to end of our journey, you should have some tools in your toolbelt to help you dramatically improve the experience your customers have with you. Once you begin the process of implementation, you will begin seeing changes on the face of your customers and in the morale of the people around you.

I want you to now approach everything you do in business based on whether you are doing it with the 6th star in mind. You will never again be able to look at any business with 5-star eyes. You are now forever destined to hold yourself and others to a higher standard of service excellence.

Remember, attaining the 6th star has nothing to do with the traditional rating systems that currently exist in the world. It a philosophy and a lifestyle that will seep into every fiber of your body until you are oozing with the desire to take immaculate care of each one of your precious customers.

How about if you and I make a pact right now? Let's commit to operating our businesses based on the 6-Star Service Manifesto and see if we can begin to influence others to make the same commitment to their customers.

Who knows? One day, we may scrap the 5-Star system altogether and replace it with one that holds businesses to a higher level of professionalism, service excellence, and keeping our customers happy!

One of the main frustrations in a book like this is implementation.

So many of us attend seminars and read books to improve our business, but never take action. We can be highly motivated and agree wholeheartedly with the need to change, but the busyness of our operations can push needed changes into corners.

Let me give you some tips on implementing the 6 Stars. You may have read through the book and found multiple opportunities to make change. Certain chapters probably spoke to you more than others. Implementing the 6-Star philosophy into your business is not a linear process.

You don't have to master Star 1 before tackling the needed changes in Star 2. Improving any process in your business will ripple out and make you stand out.

One of the best strategies I have found to implementing change is something advocated by Sam Carpenter in his book, 'Work the System.'

Carpenter is a systems thinker and is committed to creating self-sustaining systems and processes in his business. Most businesses recreate the wheel every day and don't have a consistent process to help with daily, weekly, and monthly tasks. This frustrates people and can make your business erratic at best.

When you stand back and look over all the potential changes you want to make in the way you deal with customers, it can be tough to know where to start.

Sometimes, it is best to pick an item and begin rather than stew over your list for days and weeks without implementing any changes.

We have talked about finding a customer's pain and using that to create high quality CS. Turn that strategy upon yourself. Look for the areas in your business where your CS processes are creating the most pain for people and start there. If something is screaming at you right now in your business, use that as a starting point to make changes.

Attaining the 6th Star is not something that happens once, then you never have to worry about it again. It's something that you need to work hard at and recreate each day. The good news is that you will NEVER have the same approach to taking care of your customers again. You are now forever a proud card-carrying member of the **"6-Star Club,"** never again to be associated with the lowly 5-Star folks.

For that, I say congratulations, and I wish you luck with your new set of eyes!

A SPECIAL THANK YOU NOTE

I truly appreciate you taking the time to invest in your quality of life, your business, and your future! If you found the book to be beneficial, I would be grateful if you would leave a 5-Star review on Amazon. It would mean the world to me!

Looking for more inspiration and actionable tools to grow your business and design your perfect lifestyle? Then subscribe to the hottest new show the "Business Edge Radio" Podcast with Mitche Graf on iTunes, Stitcher, Google Play, Spotify, and others. Hear dynamic interviews with world-class Entrepreneurs as well as regular dose of meat-and-potatoes techniques that will ignite your superpower to achieve even greater things!

Additional resources can be found at www.MitcheGraf.com.

Thank you for spending this time with me, and good luck with your new set of eyes!

Sources

1

https://www.superoffice.com/blog/customer-service-benchmark-report/

2

https://www.accenture.com/t20150527t210356__w__/mx-es/_acnmedia/accenture/conversion-assets/dotcom/documents/local/es-la/pdf/accenture-global-consumer-pulse-research-mexico-retail-banking-2012.pdf

3

https://www.entrepreneur.com/article/228129#ixzz2dtg5wBrf

4

https://michaelhyatt.com/wp-content/uploads/2017/06/MH-Strategic-Relationship-Matrix-2017.pdf

5

https://www.warbyparker.com/culture

6

https://bthechange.com/from-prison-tech-to-educational-museum-companies-that-redefine-customer-service-e8204964f2f0

7

https://www.ritzcarlton.com/en/about/gold-standards

8

https://hbr.org/2018/10/6-ways-to-build-a-customer-centric-culture

9

https://www.zappos.com/about/stories/record-call

10

https://www.bbc.com/news/business-16812545

11

https://www.shankman.com/the-greatest-customer-service-story-ever-told-starring-mortons-steakhouse/

12

https://www.dailymail.co.uk/news/article-2241454/Now-thats-customer-service-Lego-tracks-rare-train-set-Aspergers-boy-11-saved-years-discover-longer-made.html

13

https://www.twincities.com/2013/01/23/60-years-after-teens-complaint-pearsons-candy-co-makes-it-right/

14

https://transcosmos.co.uk/blog/best-customer-service-stories-ever-2013/

15

https://www.godvine.com/read/halo-help-142.html

16

https://www.pharmacytimes.com/news/kroger-pharmacist-dispenses-monster-repellent-to-child

17

https://www.inc.com/chris-matyszczyk/delta-vs-ann-coulter-where-do-you-stand.html

18

https://www.reddit.com/r/AskReddit/comments/1fel08/what_company_has_such_good_customer_service_that/ca9kiyn

19

https://www.mirror.co.uk/news/uk-news/mans-hilarious-complaint-aldi-defective-6428801

20

https://www.nytimes.com/2013/03/10/your-money/a-whirlpool-microwave-and-a-customer-service-problem.html

21

https://www.thedrive.com/news/25074/performance-shop-crashes-customers-audi-s4-denies-obligation-to-pay-for-repairs

Made in the USA
Coppell, TX
08 August 2021

60148900R00108